ANALYTICS
FOR
BUSINESS SUCCESS

A GUIDE TO ANALYTICS FITNESS™

By

Hema Seshadri, Ph.D.

Copyright © Hema Seshadri, Ph.D. 2023
All Rights Reserved.

ISBN 979-8-88935-817-6

This book has been published with all efforts taken to make the material error-free after the consent of the author. However, the author and the publisher do not assume and hereby disclaim any liability to any party for any loss, damage, or disruption caused by errors or omissions, whether such errors or omissions result from negligence, accident, or any other cause.

While every effort has been made to avoid any mistake or omission, this publication is being sold on the condition and understanding that neither the author nor the publishers or printers would be liable in any manner to any person by reason of any mistake or omission in this publication or for any action taken or omitted to be taken or advice rendered or accepted on the basis of this work. For any defect in printing or binding the publishers will be liable only to replace the defective copy by another copy of this work then available.

Interior graphics designed using images from freepik.com.

Table of Contents

Acknowledgments

I want to thank Mark Aisenberg, Dr. Varshaa Ashish, Dr. Bridget Cole, Louis Frolio, Jan Galkowski, Bijoy Ghosh, David Hassler, Kenneth Hu, Joseph Kambourakis, Dr. Vinay Kanitkar, Dr. Carl Lovely, Torbjorn Ose, Dr. Krishna Seshadri, Justin Sheehy, P.N. Suryanarayanan, Joanne Southwell, Dr. Chandrasekaran Srinivasan, Dr. Nancy Totah and Jean Wiley for mentorship, guidance, sponsorship and friendship over various facets of my scientific and engineering careers.

Chapter 1

Introduction

Analytics in a business setting is a methodology that uncovers patterns and associated practical information from data to drive future business decisions. While it is possible to gain business insights from informed *exploratory data analysis,* the term *analytics* is reserved for deeper assessments that provide automatic or semiautomatic insights.[1] Analytics provides concise information about the state of organizational processes and systems and yields metrics that enable fact-based decision-making. It furnishes opportunities to plan and optimize efficiency while reducing the costs of organizational systems and processes (*Fig. 1*).

Fig. 1: Analytics

Why is this important? In today's world, the primacy of data is clear and inescapable. The advent of mobile, networking, cloud computing and Big Data technologies has ushered in an analytics revolution. This ongoing transformation is of such wide-ranging scope, scale, and impact that it is being labeled by many as the Fourth Industrial Revolution, or Industry 4.0 (*Fig. 2*). The steam engine (Industry 1.0) powered the dawn of industry in the 18th century, the age of science, electricity, and mass production (Industry 2.0) accelerated its growth, and the emergence of digital technology (Industry 3.0) led to the profound advances of the information age. Now, Industry 4.0 is producing innovations that would have been inconceivable just a decade ago.

---

1   Tukey. *Exploratory Data Analysis.* Pearson, 1977.

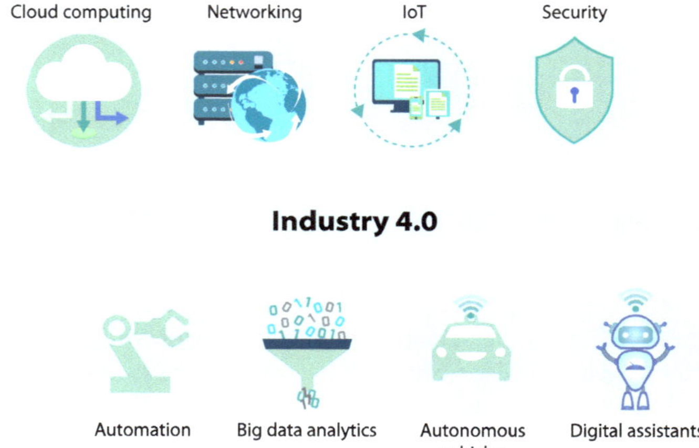

Fig. 2: Fourth Industrial Revolution, Industry 4.0

Even a cursory glance at today's technology and business landscape reveals the centrality of data to innovation and growth. The *Internet of Things (IoT)*—a network of connected devices with built-in sensors and actuators that generate raw data and talk to each other—is not science fiction anymore (*Fig. 3*). Robots have already made their mark by improving productivity in many industries, from automotive to agriculture, health care and public security. E-commerce giants already use automation in warehouses to fulfill orders with greater reliability, accuracy, speed, efficiency, compliance, and cost savings.

Meanwhile, autonomous intelligent machines are being built with Radio Frequency Identification (RFID) tags, sensors, or RFID-sensor combinations used in conjunction with actuators, data, and advanced analytics. And these advances are just the beginning.

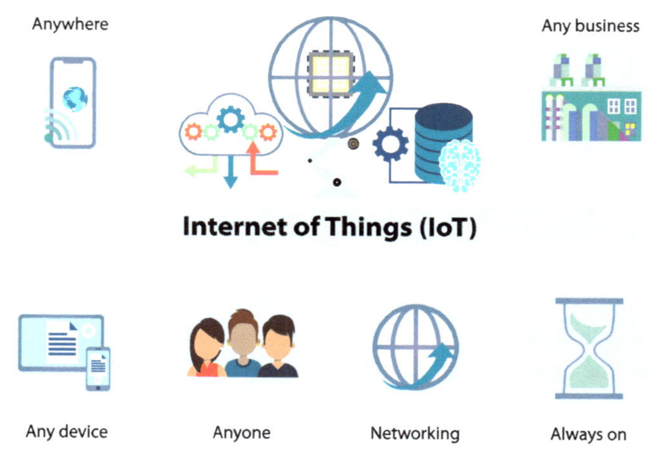

Fig. 3: Connected devices, Internet of Things (IoT)

Perhaps nowhere is the data ecosystem having a greater impact than in business. Analytics—the key to deriving value from data—is helping companies probe deeper, uncover business insights, and make smarter and faster decisions that make a real difference to their productivity and growth. It is now relatively common for businesses of all sizes to use data and analytics (D&A) to gain precise insights, make evidence-based decisions, reduce operational expenditures, improve the customer experience, and increase market share and profitability.

And these efforts have only been accelerated by the COVID-19 pandemic. According to a 2020 report published by global consulting firm CapGemini, about 67% of organizational leaders today actively promote the use of AI, IoT, cloud computing, and Big Data technologies (*digital transformation*).[2] The report goes on to say that such digital transformation initiatives have grown by 32% since 2018, largely due to the pandemic.

Supply chain management, for example, is one area in which analytics is utilized extensively to monitor end-to-end processes. Supply chain networks powered by analytics can span an organization's various locations, as well as multiple organizational verticals or business units, such as sales, operations, finance, manufacturing, marketing, and engineering. Analytics provides actionable insights across the supply chain, from demand forecasting to order fulfillment (*Fig. 4*). It also aids in the management of inventory levels, warehouse logistics, demand planning and vendor orchestration, and the optimization of transportation and delivery costs, staffing and risk mitigation.

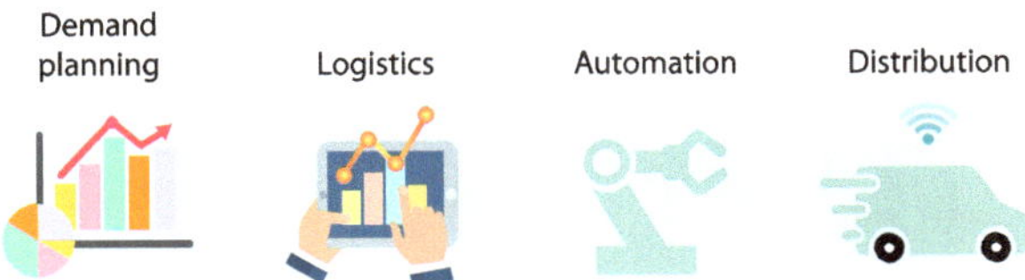

Supply Chain Management (SCM)

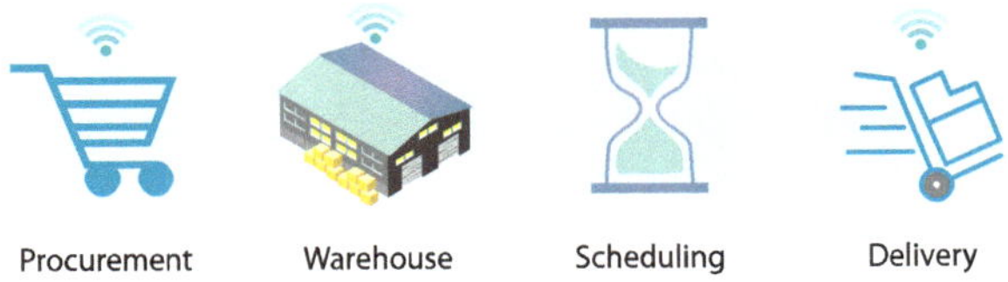

Fig. 4: Supply chain management – factory-to-customer pipeline

---

2   https://www.capgemini.com/wp-content/uploads/2020/10/IDC-MarketScape-Worldwide-Business-Analytics-Consulting-and-System-Integration-Services-Vendor-Assessment-2020.pdf

In 2006, Clive Humby, a British mathematician, coined the phrase *"Data is the new oil."* Since then, *"Data is the new gold,"* and *"Data is the new currency,"* and other iterations of the slogan have emerged as market commentators attempt to capture and convey the immense importance of data in the evolving economic landscape. According to a 2020 report published by *The Economist*, data is worth up to two trillion dollars in the US market.[3] We no longer need to convince the naysayers who ask, *"Why is data important?"* The value of data is now a given. Data has won the battle for cultural relevance.

Despite the ubiquity and importance of data and analytics in business, however, implementing a digital transformation in an organization is far from a simple task. Here are some sobering statistics:

- 87% of data science projects never make it to production (VentureBeat, 2019)[4]
- 85% of Big Data projects fail (Gartner, 2019)[5]
- 80% of analytics projects will be inadequately operationalized and poorly understood in the organizations where they are introduced, being viewed as alchemy run by wizards whose talents will not scale (Gartner, 2019)

This book will examine why the vast majority of digital transformations fail and will present some steps businesses can take to overcome the hurdles often encountered when launching an analytics project or a data initiative in a business setting.

"But aren't those issues covered in the books I've already read?" you might ask. The truth is that the technical books in the marketplace are thorough in their coverage of the technical challenges posed by advanced analytics projects, but they fail to address the organizational cultural challenges engineers, management, and key decision-makers may need to overcome to bring their projects to fruition. After all, *most business problems are people and process problems.*

This book is not among the plethora of technical deep-dive books on data and analytics technology geared towards software engineers and machine learning gurus. It is not an advanced analytics how-to guide, promising immediate results and a high return on investment. Nor does it resemble the many business articles and marketing blogs that dwell on dazzling success stories involving artificial intelligence (AI), machine learning (ML), Big Data, and Internet of Things (IoT) technologies. It is not intended as a textbook or manual on how to do analytics in a business setting. Rather, this book is an overview aimed at piquing your curiosity about the subject and opening the door to an understanding of the many ways in which analytics can support your business goals. You may be looking to:

- Find creative ways to unlock efficiencies and continue the growth trajectory of your business by increasing revenue and reducing operational costs.

---

3   https://www.tomdavenport.com/getting-serious-about-data-and-data-science/
4   https://venturebeat.com/2019/07/19/why-do-87-of-data-science-projects-never-make-it-into-production/
5   https://blogs.gartner.com/andrew_white/2019/01/03/our-top-data-and-analytics-predicts-for-2019/

- Explore conservative but effective methods to facilitate organizational analytics transformations, pivoting from ad hoc to automated analytics.
- Question the organizational status quo and push boundaries.
- Test the waters and consider how data-enabling advanced analytics and AI could become a critical part of your organization's strategic planning.
- Deepen your understanding of automation, machine learning (ML), Big Data, IoT, cloud computing, and data management to keep up with the fourth industrial revolution (Industry 4.0).

As an introduction to data analytics and artificial intelligence (a form of advanced analytics) in business, this book focuses on the preconditions and processes needed for the successful implementation of analytics transformation projects. It presents a simple and easy-to-follow analytics paradigm that is relevant to employees across all facets of an organization and provides a common language through which they can effectively communicate, share ideas, and advance the organization's analytics goals.

From this book, you will learn how to initiate analytics projects in your organization from scratch. The book will take you through the necessary steps to move from successful ad hoc to automated analysis. It will also familiarize you with the various components of the analytics life cycle, such as data collection, cleaning, processing, formatting, and storage, and the development of analytic methods, scientific techniques, and automated tools.

This book is suitable for people of all disciplinary backgrounds. It is intended to provide useful insights to managers and aspiring managers who may have no prior experience or knowledge of analytics, software, or data technologies.

If you are an executive or an aspiring executive looking to build robust, continuously evolving analytics and refine business processes to reduce costs, this book is for you. If you are a manager or an aspiring manager and you want to deploy analytics in production to enhance productivity and ongoing business value, this book is for you. If you are curious about analytics, interested in using analytics to solve challenging business problems, or looking to take your existing analytics efforts to the next level, and willing to learn, adapt and evolve, this book is for you.

This book concentrates on the fundamentals of analytics—principles, concepts, new technologies, and techniques that can allow an organization to incorporate data-driven decision-making into their current workflows and processes. This book does not go into deep technical details about machine learning, data architecture, Big Data, or statistics. Instead, it covers the basic ingredients of the field to enable managers to be active participants in analytics projects.

The goal of this book is to equip you with a systematic approach to analytical thinking that will enable you to apply creativity and domain knowledge to analytics projects in your organization. It is also intended to motivate and empower you to take the initiative and relish the challenge of the valleys, detours, and occasional roller coaster rides you may encounter as you explore the rapidly evolving world of analytics.

Chapter 2

Why Link Analytics and Business?

Non-technology organizations that reached their apex in the 2000s or early 2010s made it to the pinnacle without needing to capitalize on data and analytics or Big Data technology. The executives who climbed the ranks, under pressure to keep their businesses afloat and profitable while balancing demands from their boards and juggling competing priorities, tended to rely on what they knew, which was usually not analytics *(Fig. 5)*

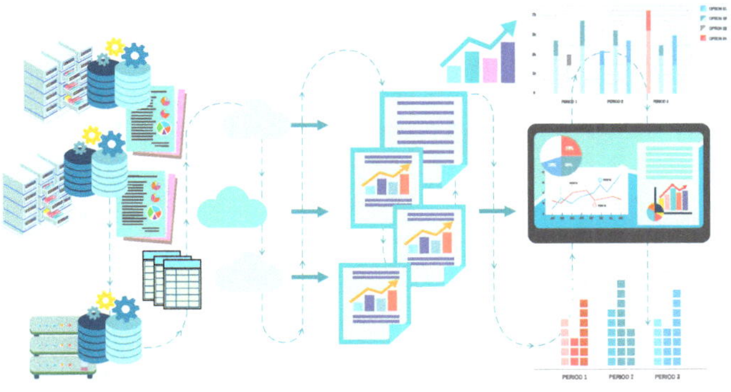

Fig. 5: Deriving business insights from data

Today, however, the days of going on gut instincts alone to steer an organization to success are firmly in the rear-view mirror. Top tech companies, which have become the dominant actors in our economy, have centered their core business on advanced analytics. Analytics and AI provide them with the tools to build intelligence around customer data that they use to improve the customer experience, maintain market share, and—in some cases—beat their forecasts, despite the economic downturn fueled by the COVID-19 pandemic. Thanks to popular business reviews and marketing blogs, yesterday's statisticians have been replaced by the data scientists and ML engineers of today.

But what, precisely, is it that analytics offers business leaders and managers? And why has analytics become an indispensable tool in the quest for organizational transformation? To answer these questions, let us look at what data analytics is and examine the increasingly sophisticated capabilities it affords companies that manage to effect a successful digital transformation.

What Is Data Analytics?

Data analytics broadly refers to scientific thinking, experimentation, and validation techniques that are applied to data streams and blended with technological advancements and automation. Analytics models attempt to translate real-world phenomena into mathematical relations by finding and extracting hidden patterns, relationships, or trends in data.

The process of assimilating real-world relationships (represented by data sets whose relationships and logic are defined by an algorithm) into a model (modeling, or model development) is a pivotal part of the Analytics Product Life Cycle (APLC). Analytics models—whether they focus on examining historical behaviors, mimicking real-world scenarios, or optimizing complex processes—can ultimately yield insights capable of revolutionizing every aspect of a business's strategy and processes. They can only do so, however, if they are successfully operationalized and if the data and insights they generate are effectively embedded in the organization's processes and workflows to drive decision-making at every level.

In a business setting, being data-driven simply means making better business decisions with insights generated from data. A data-driven culture uses a combination of exploratory data analysis (EDA) and advanced analytics techniques to discover rich insights that have both strategic and tactical implications. Data is used to inform and influence organizational business strategy. Data feeds reports, and reports promote deeper analysis, discussion, and actionable insights. Business leaders incorporate key findings to influence and set the organization's directional goals. This provides value and accelerates profitability (*Fig. 6*).[6]

The Analytics Value Chain

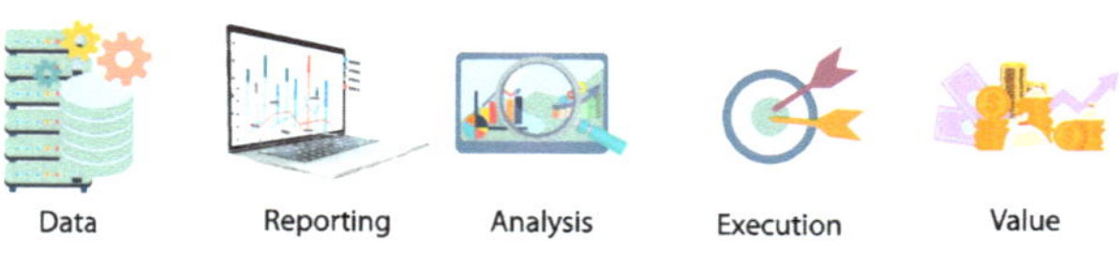

Fig. 6: Analytics value chain

---

6   https://blog.adobe.com/en/publish/2010/10/19/reporting-vs-analysis-whats-the-difference

Analytics can be divided into three categories: descriptive, predictive, and prescriptive[7] (*Fig. 7*). While descriptive analytics, or operational analytics, is classified as *business intelligence* (BI), prescriptive and predictive analytics are collectively known as *advanced analytics and AI*. Here, we will outline the characteristics and capabilities of each of the three analytics categories.

Descriptive: What is happening in my business? What should I do now?	**Predictive:** What could happen?	**Prescriptive:** What do I need to do?
Provides a comprehensive view of the business. • Reporting/Alerts/Ad hoc reports: What actions are needed? What is the problem? How many? How often? When?	Facilitates "learning" from historical data. • Predictive modeling: Predict future probability and trends. • Statistical modeling: Uncover unseen data patterns, interactions, and relationships.	Enables balancing of constraints and furnishes informed insights as a basis for recommendations to decision-makers. • Optimization: What is the best course of action? • Simulation: What will happen if we try this?

Fig. 7: Analytics categories

Descriptive Analytics, the entry point in the analytics taxonomy, seeks answers about *what is happening now or has happened in the past*. In the case of a hospital management system (*Fig. 8*), for example, descriptive analytics can tell us how many hospital beds remain open in a COVID-19 ward. It can also determine how many doctors, nurses and medical technicians are available to treat patients, and how much essential equipment is required.

Predictive Analytics, at level two in the analytics taxonomy, enables organizations or businesses that can do descriptive analytics to leap forward and address what is likely to happen in the future. In our hospital management example, predictive analytics can tell us when we will run out of hospital beds if we remain on our current course. It can also calculate how many nurses and doctors we will need to hire to maintain sufficient staffing levels and standard of care.

Prescriptive Analytics, which sits at the top of the advanced analytics taxonomy, seeks to answer, "*What should I do now?*" Or "*How should I do it?*" Referring once again to our

---

7   Lustig I, Dietrich B, Johnson C, Dziekan C (2010) The Analytics Journey, *Analytics Magazine*, 11–18. Available at https://www.crystalballservices.com/Research/Articles-on-Analytics-Risk/business-analytics-going-the-distance

hospital management example, prescriptive analytics tells us what corrective actions we will need to take to avoid running out of hospital beds.

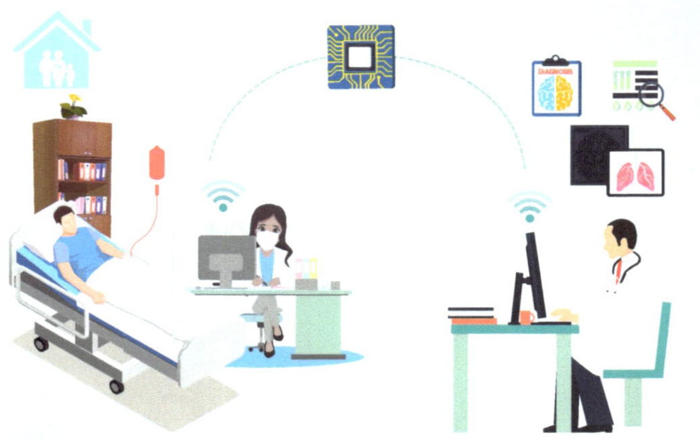

Fig. 8: Representation of hospital management system

Now we will explore each level in the analytics taxonomy in a little more detail and look at the possibilities each offers in the business environment.

Descriptive Analytics

As we have observed, descriptive analytics seeks answers about *"What is happening now?"* or *"What has happened in the past?"* It provides measurable information about the state of an organization or process. It is used to examine and evaluate day-to-day operations and historical trends, and to provide snapshots of an organization's operations and workflows.

The origins of descriptive analytics and BI—essentially, Analytics 1.0—can be traced back to the 1950s.[8] That was the era when customer transactions and data from manufacturing and production processes were first collected, aggregated, analyzed, and used in a systematic fashion to deliver fact-based understanding that removed the element of intuition or guesswork from decision-making. Organizations initiated descriptive analytics and BI projects simply by collating their existing organizational data in spreadsheets. Since then, descriptive analytics has come a long way. Its success and high adoption rates can be partially attributed to the development of data repository technologies introduced in the 1980s and to subsequent advances like today's widespread availability of handy and inexpensive commercial "software as a service" solutions.

The data collected through descriptive analytics can be summarized and presented visually using graphical techniques (exploratory data analysis, or EDA) such as charts and graphs, which can help uncover hidden structures within the data and identify exceptions and

---

8   https://hbr.org/2013/12/analytics-30

anomalies. Descriptive analytics can take the form of visually appealing and intuitive dashboards or reports that measure the performance of various business verticals and functional groups. It can be used to compare the performance of groups that handle revenue, sales, marketing, manufacturing, and engineering against business objectives.

Descriptive analytics and EDA are often used for ad hoc analysis, management consultant projects, or operational dashboards. They permit users to drill down or roll up organizational data to diagnose faults and exceptions or simply to get a pulse check of the state of the business's operational performance or strategic initiatives.

Descriptive analytics is considered the presentation layer of advanced analytics. It hides the foundational nuts and bolts of higher-order ML, data engineering and software engineering, architecture, and statistics. All the heavy lifting (*plumbing, janitorial*) and foundational work happen behind the scenes.

While descriptive analytics requires certain prerequisites to be in place, it does not require the extensive advance work necessitated by higher-order advanced analytics. Business problems must be accurately framed and corporate or external data from various data streams must be collected, collated, automated, and organized in a consistent format with the help of a unified analytics platform (UAP) before a descriptive analytics project can be started. At the upper echelons of the analytics taxonomy, by contrast, much more groundwork is needed. For predictive and prescriptive analytics projects, foundational data and analytics (D&A) components must be assembled, new research ideas must have time to percolate, and purpose-built, state-of-the-art analytics platforms and models will likely need to be developed.

As the most accessible rung of the analytics ladder, descriptive analytics has been widely adopted across the business landscape. Descriptive analytics projects can get off the ground quickly and present an easy learning curve for organizations with decades of experience in creating management reports and working with structured data. The low cost of descriptive analytics technologies, coupled with the low threshold to entry with respect to the technical skill set or analytics sophistication required of its users, has made descriptive analytics a top priority for organizations in most industries.

The utility and widespread adoption of descriptive analytics is reflected in survey results published in 2022 by the market research firm Shibuya Data Count, showing that (based on data collected from top technology leaders such as Dell, Microsoft, IBM, Oracle, Accenture, TCS, Infosys, SAP, etc.) the global descriptive analytics market is projected to show a compound annual growth rate of 18% between 2022 and 2031.[9]

It is now the widespread expectation in the business environment that decisions will be based on data and facts, not intuition alone. This fundamental shift in organizational

---

9   https://www.benzinga.com/pressreleases/22/02/25771304/descriptive-analytics-market-2022-introduction-definition-specifications-classification-and-industr

thinking—aided by technological advances in data, software, storage technology, and solutions—has enabled organizations to become data-smart, accelerate growth, and secure a competitive edge in the marketplace.

Predictive Analytics

Predictive analytics, the middle level in the analytics taxonomy *(Fig. 9)*, is often referred to as strategic analytics. It allows organizations to use data to outline business strategy and plan proactively for market disruptions or changes in customer behavior. Predictive analytics models have this power because they can estimate an unknown target variable—in other words, an unknown future value (prediction)—based on underlying patterns and anomalies that they detect in business data.

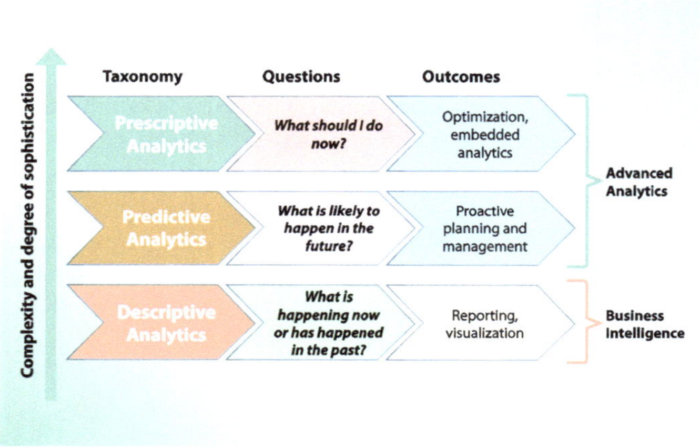

Fig. 9: Analytics categories

Predictive analytics uses a combination of data architecture, data processing, statistics, mathematical models, and ML techniques to factor in past events, implicit dependencies, relationships, associations, and conditions defining past events. It unveils business risks and opportunities by collating hidden patterns, growth trends, anomalies, and exceptions in past business transactions into model approximations and assumptions.

Predictive analytics can drive strategic corporate initiatives and decision-making on current events. It is used to predict the drop-off of high revenue–generating customers, to manage customer loyalty proactively, or to inform an organization's marketing strategy or trigger its decision to explore new markets. It can monitor shifts in customer product consumption patterns and guide the introduction of new products tailored to customer demographics. It can be used to determine incentives that correspond to customers' wants, needs and preferences, once they have been accurately grouped based on specific traits (interests, habits) or factors (demographics, industry, income). In the package and product delivery segments, it improves the customer experience by overhauling supply chain management (SCM). It is used in predictive maintenance by foreseeing machine failures in manufacturing, disk failures in storage industries, and component failures in SCM.

In the financial services industry, predictive analytics can detect counterfeit credit cards, stolen credit cards, identity theft, and money laundering. Predictive analytics facilitates fraud detection by predicting the outcome measurement, also called a dependent variable. In the case of a fraud detection system, the result, outcome, or dependent variable is either a fraudulent transaction or a non-fraudulent transaction.

In the healthcare and life insurance industries, falsified medical records, fake injuries, fake deaths, murders, or black-market prescription drugs can be detected by predictive analytics. While this capability may seem mysterious and magical, the underlying systems simply use data—such as a business's past service usage, a patient's vitals, a customer's spending patterns, or other inputs—to model an outcome.

Irrespective of an industry's size or vertical, managers want to forecast revenue precisely, deploy human resources efficiently, inventory accurately, and achieve favorable returns on investments (ROI). Predictive analytics is the ideal tool to achieve each of these goals. With predictive analytics, it is even possible to forecast an organization's probability of success based on its key performance indicators (KPI) and metrics.

Predictive analytics generates knowledge that can be used to plan, pivot, and course-correct rapidly when issues are detected, to maintain a competitive edge in the marketplace. It is used heavily in inventory planning, manufacturing, finance, healthcare, hospitality, and law enforcement. Most organizations, however, have yet to leap from using descriptive analytics/BI to harnessing the power of advanced analytics.

Prescriptive Analytics

Prescriptive analytics is the upper echelon in the advanced analytics taxonomy. It seeks to find the optimal answers to questions like, *"What should I do now?" "How should I do it?"* or *"What changes should we make to improve things?"*

Prescriptive analytics uses predictive analytics fundamentals to prescribe suitable corrective actions or new solutions via the simulation of various business scenarios. It suggests best options to follow or explore, facilitates strategic decision-making, and is often used for allocating scarce resources. As such, it represents a significant shift from descriptive analytics, which is exploratory in nature. In some cases, there is no clear line between predictive and prescriptive analytics.

Prescriptive analytics problems typically materialize in the course of descriptive and predictive analytics projects. In short, prescriptive analytics is considered the final frontier in computational intelligence and analytics, and it outlines specific interventions based on its predictions.

Let us explore a few key concepts and techniques related to predictive and prescriptive analytics: simulation, optimization, and linear programming.

What is Simulation?

Simulation refers to the process of modeling a real-life scenario using computers. Different hypothetical scenarios are simulated to study how a system works with various inputs or designs. By changing variables in mathematical simulation models according to expert *heuristics,* we can generate predictions. Model results can facilitate critical business decision-making and can suggest corrective actions to mitigate risk for products, processes, and infrastructure.

Simulation is used in various industries, such as finance, manufacturing, supply chain management, and engineering. Performing a simulation is an inexpensive way to conduct an experiment with minimal risk. The technique is used in decision support systems for problem-solving and replicating real-life scenarios. For instance, simulation is used in amusement parks to reduce bottlenecks for popular rides. In supply chain management, it is used for inventory planning and reducing transportation costs.

What is Optimization?

Identifying and choosing the correct (optimal) product from various available options involves a process called *optimization.* In mathematical optimization, a "cost," "loss," or "error" function quantifies the amount of deviation (error) between predicted and actual outcomes. Optimization strategies aim to minimize the cost function.

Optimization problems, which identify the best possible outcomes from a set of alternatives, present a set of constraints and a measure of "best" as possible inputs. They are often used to answer practical questions:

- How can we do things better?
- What is the best solution given various constraints and a variety of feasible solutions?

Optimization can either maximize or minimize possible outcomes, according to a predetermined goal. An ensemble of optimization models, including linear programming, integer and mixed-integer programming, nonlinear programming, and stochastic programming are used to solve optimization problems. Linear programming is the best known of these techniques.

What is Linear Programming?

In linear programming, the inputs to the mathematical model and the requirements and formulation of the problem at hand are depicted in a linear relationship. The discipline of linear programming has been around for several decades and has been used in a variety of business settings and other situations. The ease with which it can provide optimal solutions to seemingly unsolvable, complex decision problems makes it one of the most common and popular optimization techniques. Listed below are examples where linear programming has been used in the context of prescriptive analytics:

- Finding a feasible combination of environmental alternatives that minimize the emissions of transport fleets
- Planning sales force assignments based on predictions about their sales impact

- Capacity planning in stadiums for sports events
- Determining optimal hotel room prices to be published in a tour operator's brochure
- Prescribing changes to word choice in Twitter tweets to get more retweets

Let us now turn our attention to two of the most talked about—and frequently misunderstood—mathematical and statistical methods used in advanced analytics.

Artificial Intelligence and Machine Learning

Artificial Intelligence (AI)

AI is essentially the science and engineering that provides machines the ability to mimic human cognitive functioning and problem-solving skills. AI made its debut in the 1950s at Dartmouth College's AI Summer Research Project.

Since its humble beginnings, AI has made great strides, particularly in the last decade. Indeed, Andrew Ng, a leading analytics researcher, dubbed 2022 "a dazzling year in AI," referring to developments such as the release of synthetic image generator DALL-E 2 and the launch of ChatGPT, a competitor to Google's search engine optimization platform, both of which made their debut in 2022. According to Ng, the latest groundbreaking achievements in AI, including the ability to generate complex and compelling outputs such as images or paragraphs of text or code, will fuel more innovative products and research in the coming year and beyond.[10] Gartner anticipates that 30% of customers in mature markets will rely heavily on AI in their daily activities by 2023. Among other uses, AI will help consumers decide where to live, what to eat, and what to buy.[11]

Machine Learning (ML)

Machine Learning (ML), a subset or a form of AI, uses various models to *learn* from data. It takes complex data as *inputs* and derives functions (*learns* from data) to produce *outputs*. ML uses high-powered computing and mathematical models to discover and uncover hidden patterns in data without pre-programmed rules.

ML represents a fundamental departure from statistical methods, in which a statistician tests a change in research results or *dependent variables* (variables whose outcome is affected by changes to the independent variable in your data set) based on a hypothesis. ML does not require a human practitioner to first formulate a hypothesis or specify relationships between data and outcomes. Instead, ML derives the signal from the data itself. As new data is added to the ML system, the results or *output* data are continually updated without explicit programming or human intervention.

ML is extremely valuable to an organization's strategic initiatives due to its capacity to predict changes in the business and future outcomes. AI, data mining, algorithms, classification, neural networks, and deep learning (DL) are a few terms used in the context

---

10   https://www.deeplearning.ai/the-batch/issue-176/

11   https://blogs.gartner.com/andrew_white/2019/01/03/our-top-data-and-analytics-predicts-for-2019/

of ML. Both prescriptive and predictive analytics (advanced analytics) employ machine learning algorithm techniques in the model-building process.

ML was popularized in the 1990s, when IBM's Deep Blue algorithm beat reigning world chess champion Garry Kasparov in the second of two six-game chess matches.[12] Deep Blue's algorithm was programmed to learn chess concepts and attack strategies and search between 100 and 200 chess options per second based on the placement of the pieces on the chessboard. Although Deep Blue lost to Kasparov in the 1996 match, the ML algorithm was able to optimize the best chess moves and beat him in 1997. In 2011, due to technological advancements in processing speed and memory, IBM's Watson ML-based system demonstrated its ability to answer questions in natural language when it beat *Jeopardy* champion Ken Jennings.[13]

As organizations launch digital analytics transformations to increase efficiency, digitize services, automate workflows, and reduce human capital, the number of advanced analytics use cases in all industries is steadily growing. According to Algorithmia's 2020 *State of Enterprise Machine Learning* report, a survey of AI and ML use cases for small and large companies indicates that the top three top ML use cases are:

1.   Reducing company costs,
2.   Generating customer insights and intelligence, and
3.   Improving customer experience.[14]

Additional ML use cases identified in the Algorithmia study are presented below (*Fig. 10*).

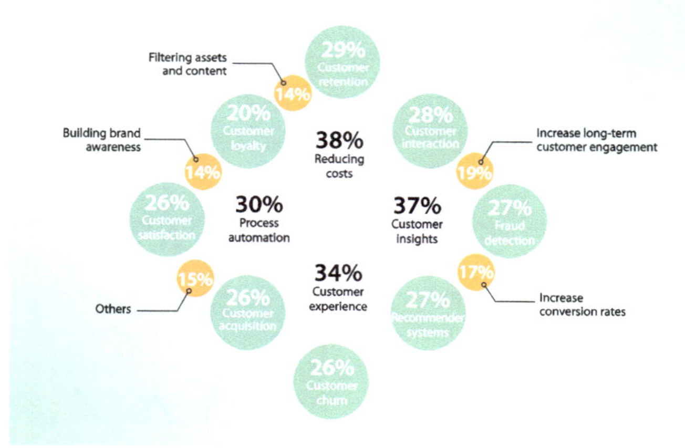

Fig. 10. Machine learning use cases and frequency

12   https://spectrum.ieee.org/the-institute/ieee-history/how-ibms-deep-blue-beat-world-champion-chess-player-garry-kasparov

13   https://www.scientificamerican.com/article/20-years-after-deep-blue-how-ai-has-advanced-since-conquering-chess/

14   https://info.algorithmia.com/hubfs/2019/Whitepapers/The-State-of-Enterprise-ML-2020/Algorithmia_2020_State_of_Enterprise_ML.pdf

While there are more than ten different types of ML problems, *supervised learning* and *unsupervised learning* are the two main types. In unsupervised learning, models can find natural groupings of data. In *supervised learning*, labeled datasets "supervise" learning by training algorithms to group data and predict outcomes.

Supervised Learning

To explain supervised learning, let's look at an analogy given by Stanford University Professors of Statistics Hastie and Tibshirani.[15] A kindergartener learns from his teacher to discriminate between a house and a tricycle. The teacher gives the child many toy houses and tricycles (training observations) in various colors and shapes. The child then learns from the labeled examples that houses have square edges and tricycles have rounded edges. The child has been given labeled training observations, and he is being supervised. If the child is given a new, previously unseen toy and is not taught whether it is a tricycle or a house, the child will draw upon his previous learnings and classify the unlabeled toy based on its features. Classification is a supervised learning method predicting outcomes based on qualitative or categorical variables. It tries to infer the output variable from a function or model that generalizes the relationship based on a set input variable.

Unsupervised Learning

Clustering and anomaly detection are two functions that fall under the category of unsupervised learning. Clustering models identify different types within a group of elements, based on the perceived characteristics of the classes. These models uncover similarities between different subsets of data and group the elements into separate clusters. They are also able to find hidden patterns not apparent to humans. They do this by finding natural groupings, data points that have more similarities to each other than to other data points in the same group. Clustering patterns change every time a task is run, accurately reflecting the different patterns of the elements in the group. Clustering can be a standalone ML algorithm used to solve a business problem or a preprocessing step implemented to produce segmented, meaningful outputs that function as inputs to other complex computations.

In business, customers can be accurately grouped based on specific traits (e.g., interests, habits) or factors (demographics, industry, income) to offer incentives personalized to their wants, needs, and preferences. Clustering models can be used to find innate natural groupings that exist in the data. What makes clustering different from a *supervised learning* problem? In classification achieved by unsupervised learning models, there is no predetermined output or target field for the model to predict. There are no standards to evaluate the accuracy of the classification, and no right or wrong answers. The benefit of clustering is its ability to capture natural groupings, supply descriptions, and identify nuances that are not possible or scalable otherwise.

---

15   James, *An Introduction to Statistical Learning: with Applications in R.* Springer, 2013.

Popular Machine Learning (ML) Problems

ML models are highly effective and can become an integral part of an organization's core business processes, strategic planning, and proactive management efforts. Classification, clustering, recommendation engines, time series analysis, text analysis, and association frequently use ML models. Rather than probing into the technical aspects of each of these processes, we will explore them via everyday examples.

Machine Learning in the Banking Industry

Let us look at a simple banking industry example. A loan officer in a local bank wants to assess a customer's risk for loan default before offering a housing loan. As inputs to the ML algorithm, he can use a gamut of variables. For example, he can input the line of credit available and the customer's credit payment history, monthly cash flows, credit score, rainy day funds, child support and divorce payments, amount in revolving credit, and current liabilities. The output is either "no" or "yes," with conditions for a credit limit, and interest rates for loan pre-approval. Here, the credit risk ML model can analyze a complex set of customer-related personal finance inputs, learn and extract information, and yield a result that helps the loan officer decide whether to offer a home loan or not.

Differentiating between possible outcomes, such as fraud vs. no fraud, risk of readmission vs. no risk of readmission, etc., is known as a classification problem.

ML in the Healthcare Industry

Advanced analytics has had a transformative influence on the healthcare industry. Hospitals striving to address rising healthcare costs while still building and maintaining patient trust count on advanced analytics to improve business efficiencies. On the patient care coordination front, advanced analytics is used for automated prescription refills, automated customer care (to reduce bottlenecks), shared electronic health records (EHR) for better diagnostics, and appointment reminders (to reduce patient no-shows).

The incorporation of preventive care as an integral part of healthcare system processes is one essential application. Proactively monitoring patient health, lifestyles, and disease management eventually reduces the cost of healthcare. It is possible to sort patients that are high-risk and predict the chances of recurring hospital visits or high co-morbidity rates due to preexisting health conditions. Advanced analytics is leveraged in the healthcare industry in myriad ways to improve the standard of care while simultaneously refining process optimization to reduce operational costs. Applications range from tracking healthy living habits and disease prevention factors to identifying patterns related to disease progression, to determining the optimal ratio of nurses and doctors to patients.

On the medical diagnostics front, predictive analytics augments a clinician's complex decision-making processes. Clinicians can use predictive analysis to detect the early signs of health deterioration of at-risk patients with existing comorbidities, such as diabetes, asthma, and heart disease.

ML can also be used to help healthcare experts classify benign vs. cancerous tissue. How is this done? Oncologists and radiologists have been able to blend medical domain expertise with ML and deep learning (DL) algorithms to produce computer visual analysis capable of spotting subtle patterns that the human eye might miss.[16] In radiology, computer-assisted diagnostics (CAD) has been around since the 1990s. However, the advent of *computer vision* (CV), a field of science that allows computers to "see," has been revolutionary in medical imaging.

Image detection, recognition, and identification, which comprise the CV fields of study, are used to identify leading indicators of disease and aid in diagnosis. Image *recognition* is a subfield of CV, in which a computer is given a set of images and is left to draw connections and build associations. In medical imaging, this may involve teaching (*training*) the computer with a set of images showing cancerous tissue and then permitting it to find standard features that these images have in common and that are absent in images of benign tissue, essentially allowing them to differentiate (*classify*) images (*Fig. 11*). Zebra Medical Vision's AI algorithm received FDA (Food and Drug Administration) approval in 2020 to be used in the analysis of mammograms to spot breast cancer.

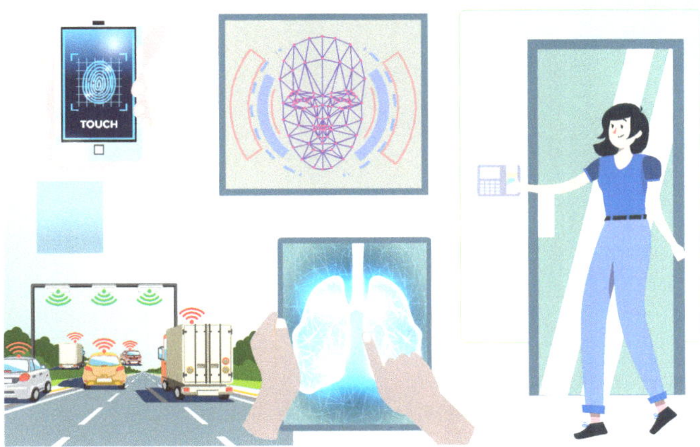

Fig. 11: Examples of CV image recognition, detection, and verification

Aside from its application in medical diagnostics, image recognition is used in other sectors, such as law enforcement, fraud detection, education, retail, and security. CV can be used to identify, detect, and verify facial features; tag photos and license plates; and detect biometric patterns from irises or fingerprints, among many other applications. In 2019 alone, 1,500 software patents were granted to facial recognition technologies, compared to six hundred in 2015.[17] If anything, this is a sign that the field of advanced analytics will only

---

16   https://www.nature.com/articles/d41586-019-03847-z

17   https://www.wipo.int/edocs/pubdocs/en/wipo_pub_1055.pdf

see continued growth, more investment, greater user adoption, and further expansion to other, untapped sectors.

Deep Learning

While ML is a subset of AI, deep learning (DL), which gained popularity around 2010, is considered a subset of the ML discipline (*Fig. 12*). DL algorithms use a function (mapping a set of inputs to a group of outputs) to extract patterns and nuances from complex datasets and identify good decision outcomes. The type of function that DL uses is represented as a neural network because the analytical calculations it uses to solve complex problems are modeled loosely on those of the human brain. The brain's neural network contains thousands, or even millions, of interconnected processing nodes (neurons) signaling one another.

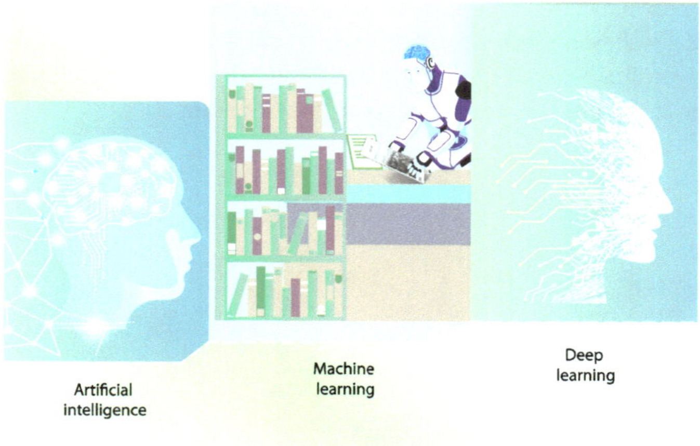

Fig. 12: Relationship between AI, ML and DL

DL requires less human intervention than its ML counterpart but needs more data and compute power. The value generated by the adoption of neural networks by top technology companies has led to DL becoming more mainstream in recent years.

The Analytics Revolution

Even this brief survey of the categories of AI and analytics provides a sense of the tremendous power of these technologies. Applied to business and industry, advanced analytics can provide a clear line of sight into organizational functioning, unearth hidden knowledge, answer questions (even questions that have not been asked yet) and predict future challenges and opportunities. It is not difficult to see why analytics is being embraced by companies around the world.

Successful analytics transformation efforts enable organizations to break disruptive operational firefighting cycles and deploy interventions to mitigate risks. They enable business managers to anticipate, plan, proactively manage, and optimize processes to reduce bottlenecks.[18] They also allow organizations to streamline operational workflows, invent, evolve, and be more resilient. The appeal of analytics to organizations recovering from the aftermath of the acute disruptions to the global supply chain catalyzed by the war in Ukraine, the COVID-19 pandemic, or other disruptions is clear.

According to a joint study performed by global consulting firm BCG (Boston Consulting Group) and MIT Sloan Management Review, globally, about fifty billion dollars were committed to AI technologies in 2020.[19] This spending was attributed to the desire of organizations to differentiate themselves in the marketplace using advanced analytics and AI. Businesses want to measure, evaluate, monitor, automate, optimize, and enhance systems and processes. They are discovering how to mine internal and external data to gain a competitive advantage. This growth in analytics capabilities, accelerated by the emergence of low-cost cloud services, innovative technologies, and wise investments, will continue in the post-COVID-19 world.

According to reports published by global consulting firm McKinsey & Company:

- Advanced analytics & AI is predicted to contribute an additional 13 trillion dollars to global GDP by 2030 (McKinsey & Company, 2022)[20]
- About two-thirds of top senior executives planned to increase their investment in advanced analytics & AI and automation efforts during the COVID-19 recovery stage. (McKinsey & Company, 2022)[21]

Organizations are scouting for new ways to secure a profitable future, one that is more resilient in the face of future unpredictable events, such as pandemics, climate change–related crises, cyber-attacks, or economic downturns. These organizations are making investments in analytics transformation efforts that will help them to prospect intelligent, nuanced ways to reimagine their risk management and mitigation strategies. Such investments are at the same time enabling them to gain more visibility into well-streamlined processes, diversify supply chains, optimize headcount, and stay competitive.

As the analytics revolution continues into the next decade, managers will be able to assimilate massive amounts of data, build a mosaic of information, and tell a story about the inner workings of their organizations, including their successes and vulnerabilities. They will become accustomed to optimizing available organizational data and mining golden nuggets of information to generate stress-free go/no-go decisions, such as whether to invest in new markets or reduce the organization's footprint.

---

18   https://hbr.org/2006/01/competing-on-analytics

19   https://www.bcg.com/press/20october2020-study-finds-significant-financial-benefits-with-ai

20   https://www.mckinsey.com/industries/public-and-social-sector/our-insights/the-potential-value-of-ai-and-how-governments-could-look-to-capture-it

21   https://www.mckinsey.com/business-functions/risk-and-resilience/our-insights/covid-19-implications-for-business

Analytics-empowered managers will preside over cycles of disruptive innovation and find solutions that will take their organizations further into the realm of advanced analytics. They will be able to uncover unexpected findings, discern relationships and associations that are nonobvious, predict the future with a high level of certainty, and optimize existing processes and solutions.

These managers will transform from information providers to insight providers. They will be expected to think abstractly and digest complex information involving monumental volumes of data. They will be required to supply bite-sized nuggets of actionable information to frontline workers. This will be the new norm. Progress, efficiency, and cost will be measured continuously by customers, stakeholders, funders, and sponsors as expectations exponentially increase. The quality of business decisions managers make based on advanced analytics projects will be measured as well. Managers' ability to succeed will depend on their willingness to stay relevant, evolve and adjust rapidly to these new demands. It will also rest on how adept they are at facilitating changes to corporate organizational culture and the way information is transmitted in the traditional, hierarchical workplace.

Data as a Horizontal™

As analytics tools and technology become readily accessible, the transformation they catalyze will do more than simply increase organizational agility and resilience. The clear line of sight they provide into organizational processes will empower workers at all tiers of an organization to take ownership of projects and steer the business toward sustainable growth.

Through this process, analytics will transform the accessibility of data from a vertical function to a *horizontal* function. *Data democratization*—the provision and dissemination of non-sensitive organizational data to workers at all levels without specialized engineering skills—will equip employees with the data they need to be highly effective in their job functions. Data democratization, aided by the self-serviceability offered by embedded analytics and user-friendly dashboards, will provide rapid data access to people with diverse expertise and skill sets at all levels. This increase in data access will create a sense of shared ownership and responsibility previously limited to the upper echelons of leadership. This shift will allow for the crowdsourcing of ideas and engage all employees involved in different aspects of an organization's business, markets, and customer service. "Rallying the troops" will enable organizations to innovate faster and gain the competitive edge offered by analytics.

Organizations that make a commitment to implementing a well-thought-out series of organizational culture and technology shifts will soon find themselves reaping the benefits of the Data as a Horizontal paradigm across every functional area of their business. This book aims to lay out some of the factors that can jump-start this transformation and move a business to the higher levels of a schema that we will refer to as Analytics Fitness.

Analytics Fitness™

Analytics Fitness is a sequence of stages that represent an organization's readiness to make informed business decisions based on the effective use of data, moving them closer to the Data as a Horizontal paradigm: the ultimate goal of Analytics Fitness. Analytics Fitness has five stages, Level-I to Level-V, each of which can be viewed as a milestone in the analytics transformation journey.

During this journey, organizations will move away from their heavy reliance on spreadsheets generated in business silos that each have a limited window on the business's data, operations, challenges, strategy, and goals. They will develop fully integrated, transparent information ecosystems, with analytics embedded in operations and processes. These information ecosystems will provide them with accurate, up-to-the-minute assessments of business performance and profitability and the ability to forecast the likely outcome of new initiatives. Organizations at the higher levels of Analytics Fitness will be equipped with the data they need to make important business decisions, chart a course for the future, and mount an agile response to black swan events.

We will learn about each Analytics Fitness level in-depth in Chapter 3 (*Analytics Fitness*), but discussion of the practical actions needed to move up the Analytics Fitness ladder will also recur in multiple places throughout this book. We will see that establishing the preconditions required to reach the upper echelons of Analytics Fitness involves a holistic transformation that spans every aspect of an organization.

What Steps Can Organizations Take to Become Data-Driven, Reach Higher Levels of Analytics Fitness and Achieve the Data as a Horizontal paradigm?

This question will form the nucleus and driving force of this book. We will see that analytics transformation can be achieved only with sufficient investment in infrastructure, software, and technology. It will be dependent upon the automation of manual, repetitive tasks, such as monitoring, notification and measurement processes. It will involve pivoting from error-prone spreadsheet management systems to automated, auditable, iterable data and analytics (D&A) solutions *(Fig. 13)*. It will mean building robust, resilient D&A infrastructure, creating automated systems to seamlessly ingest data from massive data streams, and embedding advanced analytics into organizational workflows.

Fortunately, organizations can make these investments incrementally, and see significant benefits along the way. They can also take advantage of advances in data management and analytics technologies, including cloud computing and AI products and services, that are making analytics transformation more affordable and accessible than ever before.

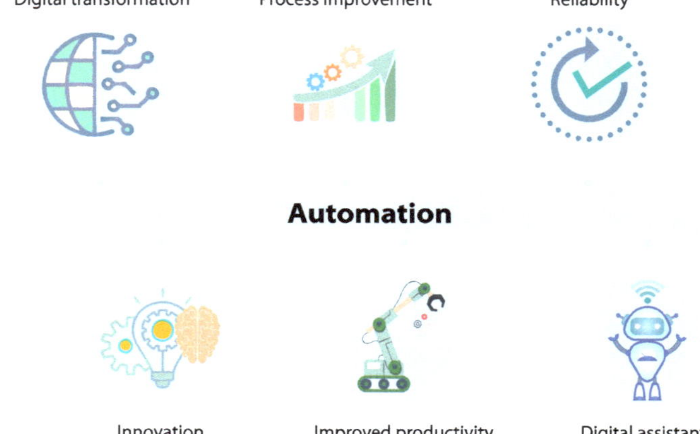

Fig. 13: Automation segments

Of course, setting up the necessary technology tools and processes is only part of the picture. As we saw in Chapter 1 (*Introduction*), despite the manifest benefits of analytics—with its potential to help organizations enjoy increased revenue, improved customer service, best-in-class operating efficiencies, and improved profitability—the vast majority of analytics projects never make it to production. As Gartner notes, even in enterprises that manage to move advanced analytics prototype models to production, only 53% are ultimately deployed.[22]

As we will see, this low success rate is often not the result of inadequate investment, or of a failure of organizational will or commitment to analytics transformation. Instead, organizations often run aground in their attempts to implement analytics projects due to a failure to do the necessary groundwork in some other key areas. Framing the right business questions, setting D&A strategy, preparing people and processes, and making the requisite changes to structure, leadership and internal culture are vital steps in facilitating analytics success. Too many organizations overlook these critical aspects of analytics readiness and fail to maximize the efficacy of their analytics projects. Incomplete or stalled analytics efforts quickly become an expensive proposition, eroding management's interest in future projects. After all, any investment must lead to tangible benefits. Process does not equal outcome.

In the coming chapters, we will look at some of the preconditions—in terms of strategy, change management, infrastructure investment and organizational housekeeping tasks—that organizations will need to put in place if they are to realize an effective analytics transformation.

---

22   https://blogs.gartner.com/andrew_white/2021/01/12/our-top-data-and-analytics-predicts-for-2021/

To Summarize:

Analytics is transforming the corporate landscape, as more organizations embrace the power of data-driven insights to further their business strategies. Data and analytics offer businesses a window into their operations, processes, markets, and customers that yields more extensive insights than were ever possible before. The analytics revolution is transforming the roles and capabilities of managers and catalyzing an overall shift toward data democratization, which has far-reaching effects on organizational structure and culture. Data as a Horizontal is a paradigm that we will refer to throughout this book. It is both an effect of analytics transformation and a desired state for organizations that wish to reap the full benefit of advanced analytics.

Analytics Fitness is a scale that measures an organization's level of readiness to implement analytics projects and the level of analytics sophistication it is capable of handling. Descriptive, predictive, and prescriptive analytics form the three major tiers of the analytics hierarchy, from the most accessible to the most complex.

Essential Takeaways:

- Implementing an analytics transformation in a business means investing in D&A infrastructure, software and automation, a process that can be done incrementally, and that will yield benefits along the way.
- Analytics transformation is not only about technology infrastructure, however. The majority of analytics projects do not make it to implementation, largely because of organizational failure to do the necessary groundwork setting D&A strategy, preparing people and processes, and making the requisite changes to structure, leadership and internal culture.
- Businesses that successfully manage both the tangible and intangible facets of analytics transformation will gain a significant competitive advantage.
- Descriptive analytics (often referred to as business intelligence, or BI) is the most accessible analytics category and has been widely deployed in business for decades.
- Predictive and prescriptive analytics are often referred to as strategic analytics or advanced analytics.
- The descriptive analytics discipline focuses on lag metrics or historical data and retrospective data analysis or exploratory analysis.
- Predictive analytics is focused on future outcomes. It can predict an unknown target variable based on underlying patterns in data.
- Prescriptive analytics uses predictive analytics fundamentals to prescribe suitable corrective actions or new solutions via simulation of various business scenarios.
- Machine learning (ML) relies on models and inferences to extract (learn) based on sample data (set of examples).
- In supervised learning, ML models are "trained" to predict outcomes (output variables) based on set input variables.

- In unsupervised learning, ML models make predictions or decisions without being given explicit instructions.
- Deep learning (DL) is a subset of the ML discipline, which is, in turn, a subset of artificial intelligence (AI).
- Advanced analytics employs ML and DL algorithm techniques in the model-building process.

Chapter 3

Analytics Fitness™

In Chapter 2 (*Why Link Analytics and Business?*), we looked at the capabilities of each of the major analytics categories—descriptive, predictive, and prescriptive (*Fig. 14*)—and the increasingly sophisticated insights companies can glean as they move up the analytics ladder. We also touched on Analytics Fitness, a scale that assesses fundamental components of an organization's progress toward the implementation of these capabilities. Organizations that wish to operate at the higher analytics levels and embrace the power of advanced analytics can only do so by moving up in the Analytics Fitness hierarchy, establishing the essential preconditions that make predictive and prescriptive analytics possible.

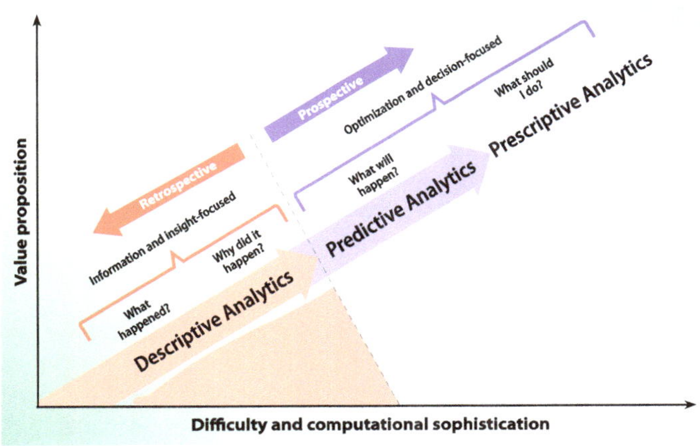

Fig. 14: Analytics hierarchy

According to a report published in 2022 by leading market intelligence firm IDC (International Data Corporation), investment in advanced analytics and AI systems will accelerate over the next several years. The compound annual growth rate for AI services is expected to reach 22% between 2022 and 2027.[23] IDC cites the fundamental impetus behind this growth as the desire to improve customer experience, enable and empower employees to be good at their jobs, transform data to deliver business outcomes at scale

---

23   https://www.idc.com/getdoc.jsp?containerId=prUS48881422

using advanced analytics and AI, and facilitate automation. The report says that digital transformation efforts and advanced analytics & AI deployment are a must for businesses that want to stay competitive.

How, then, can organizations advance toward the goal of analytics maturity[24] and reach a level of Analytics Fitness at which they can successfully navigate advanced analytics engineering projects? And how can they leverage advanced analytics & AI to transform data into knowledge and apply these findings to generate value and tangible business outcomes?

To arrive at a full understanding of what Analytics Fitness entails, we must first gain a sense of the essential components of the analytics engineering process (*Fig. 15*). The following are the phases that must be accomplished in each and every analytics project.

Analytics Engineering

1. **Problem Framing**
   - Step one involves approaching the business problem that needs solving with a goal-driven analytics mindset.

2. **Analytics Strategy**
   - Instigating an analytics strategy first involves surveying existing tools and techniques to assess the organization's current data collection, storage, management, and analytics capabilities.
   - Next, the business problem at hand should be broken into sub-components, and the tools, techniques, and data required to solve the problem should be identified.
   - Finally, a conceptual framework should be constructed, using building blocks that take into consideration business goals and organizational, technology, and resource constraints.

3. **Data Collection and Management (Unified Analytics Platform)**
   - Data collection and management are the practical building blocks of every analytics project. At this stage, data is collected, stored, and processed so it can be made available for analytics model building. Data is collected and managed according to the analytics strategy set in stage 2 of the analytics engineering process. The accomplishment of this step is heavily dependent on the existence of a Unified Analytics Platform (UAP).
   - UAP refers to the ecosystem of programming languages, packages, algorithms, cloud computing services, and general infrastructure an organization uses to collect, store, analyze, and leverage data.
   - A UAP is created by collating data from various streams and spinning off requisite data collection from internal or external third-party sources.[25]

---

24   https://www.mdpi.com/2078-2489/11/3/142/htm
25   https://online.hbs.edu/blog/post/data-ecosystem

- No two organizations leverage the same data in the same way. As such, each organization has a unique UAP. These UAPs may overlap in some cases, particularly when data is pulled or scraped from a public source, or when third-party providers are leveraged (for example, cloud storage providers).
- Building a UAP also involves deciphering, preprocessing, and cleaning the data that has been collected and building data-to-business-context associations.

4. Model Building

- At the model-building stage, engineers will develop suitable advanced analytics models that are attuned to the business problems at hand and assess the needs, data accessibility, organizational culture, and technology of the organization.
- Model testing and iteration are then done to refine the models.

5. Automation and Embedded Analytics

- At the end of the analytics engineering process, successful advanced analytics models will be enmeshed in the organization's operational processes to reach operational excellence goals.

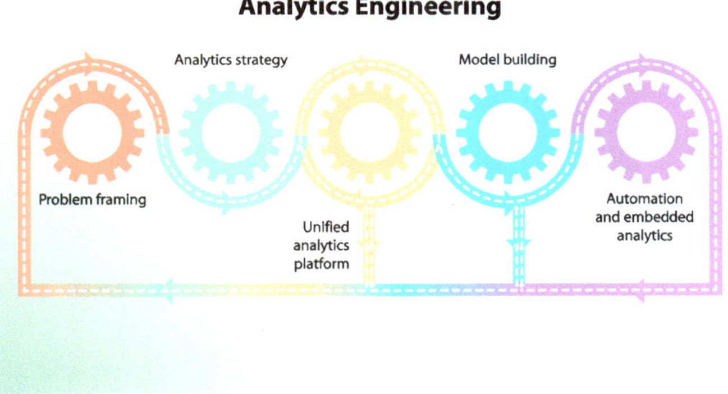

Fig. 15: Analytics engineering process

Analytics Fitness Framework™

Analytics Fitness (*Fig. 16*) consists of five levels that represent an organization's readiness to navigate the analytics engineering process and make informed business decisions through the effective use of data. As an organization reaches each successive Analytics Fitness level, it moves forward in its journey toward complete analytics and digital transformation, bringing it closer to achieving the *Data as a Horizontal* paradigm.

Analytics Fitness Level	Analytics Fitness Characteristics
Level - I	• Heavy reliance on manual reporting. • Goals/business outcomes not defined. • Unreliable, non-auditable, siloed KPIs. • Reactive decision-making. • No cohesive, organization-wide D&A strategy in place. • Poor communication between business and analytics teams. • Analytics Category: Descriptive Analytics.
Level - II	• Organizational goals (KPI) and metrics are monitored, measured in business verticals. • No cohesive, organization-wide D&A strategy in place. • Some automated reporting, alerting, and dashboarding is available but there is continued reliance on spreadsheets for data access. • Siloed data and lack of standardization of terminology and statistical methods. • Limited communication between business and analytics teams. • Analytics Category: Descriptive Analytics.
Level - III	• D&A strategy in place and aligned with organizational growth strategy. • Data somewhat standardized and terminology aligned. • Data governance practices implemented. • UAP being built. • Business outcomes clearly defined. • Clear communication between business leaders and analytics professionals. • Data context and rationalization in place. • Data available through dashboards. • Automated insights inform decision-making. • Analytics Category: Descriptive Analytics.
Level - IV	• UAP in place. • Transition from BI to advanced analytics projects in progress. • Proactive analytics planning and management. • Innovative, non-hierarchical culture that fosters collaboration. • Free flow of ideas, questions, experimentation, exploration of new ideas, and innovation. • Fail fast, learn fast approach. • Analytics Category: Predictive and Prescriptive Analytics.

Level - V	<ul><li>Optimization and simulation capabilities.</li><li>Analytics embedded in business processes.</li><li>Analytics products refined through feedback loops and iteration, capitalizing on insights from failed experimentation.</li><li>Analytics Category: Predictive and Prescriptive Analytics.</li></ul>

Fig. 16: Analytics Fitness Framework concepts

Analytics Fitness Level I

In large legacy enterprise organizations with complex workflows, technologies, and processes and no in-house analytics expertise, it will take some time to get up to speed with data and analytics (D&A). A business of this type may function at a level of reactive decision-making. These organizations typically have not invested in suitable D&A platforms and therefore do not possess the capability to take on complex analytics workloads.

Most D&A efforts in Analytics Fitness Level I fall into the keep-the-lights on category, with disparate tools and technology residing in separate business functional groups. At this level, organizations lack a cohesive D&A strategy and do not reliably disseminate organizational goals across departments. We will go into greater depth on the significance of a robust D&A strategy with clearly defined goals in Chapter 4 (*The Analytics Triad™: Goals, Metrics, and Data & Analytics Strategy*).

In organizations lacking a cohesive D&A strategy, each business vertical designs its own tools to capture and track metrics in spreadsheets and reaches its own version of the truth (OVOT). This organizational fragmentation lowers productivity and is likely to cause loss of revenue, lower profitability, and an inability to stay competitive in the marketplace. The D&A initiatives in such organizations will remain at a low level. They will typically consist of firefighting efforts using low-governance BI systems and short-lived analytics exercises that are poorly connected to business outcomes and organizational growth strategy.

Analytics Fitness Level II

Analysts or managers in organizations at the second level of Analytics Fitness are required to answer questions relevant to discrete business functions, prove or disprove theories, and propose solutions. To do this effectively, they must wrangle data and glean insights based on facts, not just experience and business acumen. The business problem statements they formulate drive decisions about the data needed and the analytics to be used in descriptive analytics projects. However, in Level II organizations, enterprise data is still spread across data silos and not tightly integrated into the business's enterprise-wide organization, operations, and processes.

Organizations at Level II lack a cohesive D&A strategy but may employ D&A strategies on an ad hoc basis within discrete functional groups. They will often use publishing and reporting dashboards that can track workflows, comment on them, communicate insights, and provide alerting capabilities. Critically, however, these organizations typically lack a Unified Analytics Platform (UAP): an ecosystem where all organizational data is democratized. As a result, there is also no standardization or alignment of data terminology or statistical methods across the organization.

Unified Analytics Platform (UAP)

A unified analytics platform (UAP)—also referred to as a data foundation or data ecosystem—stores and rationalizes all organizational data, facilitating analytics by making information accessible. A UAP helps provide ready answers to descriptive analytics questions. It also assembles raw data into a format that can be furnished as inputs to advanced analytics models. The existence of a UAP enables analytics professionals to build more complex models that may support new product releases, identify measures to increase customer loyalty and decrease churn, or otherwise further the goals of the organization.

Organizations starting out on their analytics journey should begin building a UAP. Creating a structured and well-designed analytics architecture and UAP requires investment in state-of-the-art, enterprise-level tools and technologies. Digital technology upgrades will make it possible for organizations to do automated data collection, measure performance, and monitor the state of their business and existing operational processes. These resilient digitized operations will increase reliability, reduce inaccuracies, be auditable, and not require human intervention to generate monthly, weekly, or quarterly business-specific dashboards or reports.

It is critical that the UAP be equipped with the infrastructure to support ML frameworks, statistical packages and programming languages, connectors to structured and unstructured data, cloud services, and data collection services.

As a complement to the development of a UAP, companies that aspire to advance to the higher levels of Analytics Fitness must hire talented engineers with experience in advanced analytics, cloud computing, and Big Data technologies. Other critical efforts that are often overlooked include upskilling current employees, providing information-sharing forums, and investing in self-serviceability, data literacy, and data democratization.

A robust UAP should be available to seamlessly support every step of the data life cycle *(Fig. 17)*. Learnings from completed projects, prior art, and data foundations and insights mined from each successfully completed project will provide a jumping off point for the next. We will review some of these steps in detail in Chapter 7 (*The Analytics Product Life Cycle*™).

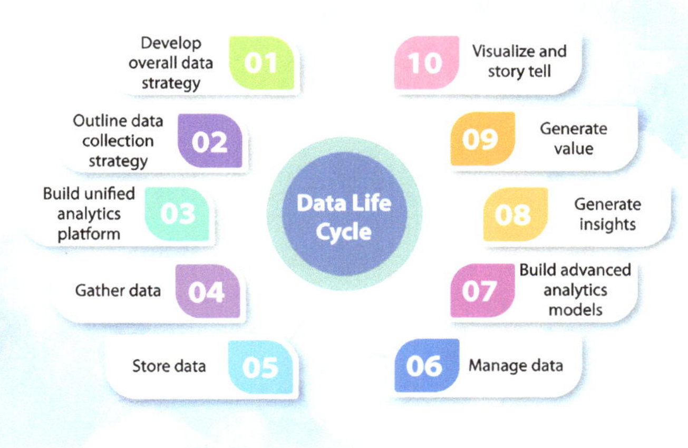

Fig. 17: Data life cycle

Investment in a UAP is critical to the success of advanced analytics initiatives. Many organizations, however, overlook the necessity of building a UAP. The absence of a UAP will likely result in "spaghetti analytics": expensive, parallel data collection, data storage infrastructure, and analytics architecture endeavors. Functional groups in organizations lacking a UAP will have to wade through troves of data from disparate business silos just to gain access to pertinent information. They will need to pore over various tools, dashboards, or spreadsheets to find optimum data connectors and tackle data reconciliation, rationalization, validation, and verification. These laborious, manual efforts will be necessary to ensure that key sources of information are identified and that the data can be consumed by analytics models.

Organizations at Level II have a low probability of being able to respond promptly to customer or executive requests, as data that is buried in silos will take time to be excavated. This organizational dysfunction may, in turn, lead to customer churn, service issues, customer incidents resulting in revenue loss, or other challenges.

Single Source of Truth

Along with the development of a UAP comes the ability to adopt rigorous data governance policies, typically based on a *single source of truth* (SSOT) paradigm. SSOT is a guideline that encourages all employees to use the same data. SSOT ensures control over quality, versions, provenance, data integrity, and regulatory compliance. Companies that aspire to become profitable and analytically competent must adopt standardization processes, automate manual workflows, and adopt a single source of truth if they are to reap increased revenues and profits. Commercial, off-the-shelf data catalog solutions are now available to help businesses maintain organizational data quality, enforce governance policies, and facilitate collaboration. Alation, Collibra, Informatica, and Immuta are popular data governance and metadata management solutions.

Level-II organizations that upgrade to a repeatable, automated framework based on a UAP will be able to effectively rationalize, validate and verify data for use in BI, descriptive analytics, and operational analytics projects. This foundation will enable them to grow into Analytics Fitness Level III.

Analytics Fitness Level III

The problems created by the lack of an overarching organizational D&A strategy are to a large extent resolved in organizations that have reached Analytics Fitness Level III. Organizations at Level III have a cohesive D&A strategy that clearly outlines the required D&A capabilities, systems and platform infrastructure and the resources required to reach their business goals.

At this level, data governance plays an important role. With clear communication between D&A wizards and business teams, these organizations will be able to identify challenges and limitations in their existing D&A platforms and find opportunities to innovate and generate business value. At Level III, organizations achieve overall alignment on D&A platform transformation efforts, D&A strategy, and organizational growth strategies.

The transition from Analytics Fitness Level II to Level III involves the extensive use of exploratory data analytics (EDA), the standardization of business terminology, and the collection of metrics in functional groups. Communications are centered around dashboards, shifting the focus from email and spreadsheets. This transition enables professionals focused on creating time-sensitive reports to seamlessly perform discovery, collate the necessary information, and tell the story. At this level, management consultants, reporting analysts, and managers shift from data consumers to experts.

Analytics Fitness Levels IV & V

The move from Analytics Fitness Level III to Level IV is fueled by the creation of a robust organizational D&A strategy and is further accelerated by the existence of a UAP.

The UAP empowers analytics professionals focused on executive management consultant projects to assess issues and propose process adjustments. Thanks to the UAP, they can finish time-sensitive tasks quickly and efficiently, leaving them much time in the day to focus on complex analysis, common themes, and trends, and on planning efforts to discover valuable insights in their domain area. This freedom to devote time and resources to exploration sets the stage for organizations to grasp the strategic potential of data. A UAP further accelerates innovation by making Big Data simple.[26] Organizations at Levels IV and V can leverage, clean, and process torrents of organizational data from previously siloed subsets of their businesses.

The transition from Analytics Fitness Level III to Analytics Fitness Level IV or V takes significant time and requires extensive experience in managing automated business decisions and incorporating AI technologies. At the higher levels of analytics

---

26   https://databricks.com/glossary/unified-data-analytics-platform

sophistication, it is critical that advanced analytics is embedded (embedded analytics) into business processes and workflows. Accomplishing this technology transformation reduces the heavy reliance on repetitive, errable, non-auditable, mundane processes that bog down less analytically advanced organizations. Embedding analytics in complex business processes and workflows allows organizations to make well-informed decisions.[27] Embedded analytics enables organizations to switch from the reactive problem-solving facilitated by reporting and reap the benefits of the proactive planning capabilities offered by predictive analytics or the sophisticated optimization recommendations presented by prescriptive analytics.

Getting to this level requires hiring highly talented, high-performing individuals who have experience in very specialized areas of advanced analytics, an entrepreneurial spirit, and impressive problem-solving skills. Investment in state-of-the-art data technologies and infrastructure is a must. This kind of transformation can be an expensive proposition for organizations with limited resources, so some organizations start with open-source software. There are plenty of great open-source product offerings in the realms of advanced analytics and Big Data from which to choose.

Fostering a culture of curiosity and cross-group collaboration, sharing domain expertise, and giving members of the organization the license to experiment and fail are mandatory for success at Levels IV and V. Encouraging out-of-the-box thinking and providing an open culture and a platform from which to speak freely and question age-old business practices is crucial. Indeed, businesses that aspire to achieve Analytics Fitness Levels IV & V will need to establish a culture in which exploring new ideas and challenging the status quo is not just encouraged but requisite for employment. This will also mean that organizations must go through a tectonic shift (if they have not done so already) from a hierarchical structure to a self-organizing, agile, and nimble one.

Providing cover for failed experimentation is vital in organizations at Analytics Fitness Levels IV & V, since not all new ideas and innovations produce immediate results or tangible gains. It is by incorporating the collective wisdom gained from such failed experiments into building better analytics products and adapting to market shifts that organizations will move closer to Analytics Fitness Level V. Eventually, an organization that ascends to this level will be become more competitive and will be able to strategize to increase market share and revenue and release new products to reach untapped demographics.

Introducing new technology and tools to mature, profitable businesses with well-established processes can be a herculean task and, at times, risky. The start-ups of the last decade and the 2020s have the competitive advantage over the industry leaders of the 2000s, since they have been able to leverage the data revolution and state-of-the-art Big Data technologies from their inception. For these innovation disruptors, AI is the core business function, not a support function, giving them an edge and the ability to leapfrog to success.

---

27   https://hbr.org/2013/12/analytics-30

At Level IV through V, organizations treat data like an organizational asset, no longer as the property of individual departments. They set up systems to collect, store, organize, and process valuable data and make it available in secure ways to the employees and advanced analytics (predictive and prescriptive) applications that need it. Then—and here's the key—they use that data to inform those all-important business decisions. Leaders need to be able to rely on solid, meaningful data to make decisions now and prepare for what's ahead.

Organizations that reach Analytics Fitness Levels IV & V, with all the requisite advances in technology, processes, and organizational culture, will find that these changes result in mutually reinforcing, transformational shifts. Data becomes an accessible organizational asset, available to foster further, continuous evolution and achieve the Data as a Horizontal paradigm. As data is democratized, no longer hoarded in individual departments or tightly controlled in hierarchical fiefdoms, the gap between knowledge workers and advanced analytics practitioners will decrease. The democratization of data will fuel ongoing innovation and collaboration that, in turn, will keep the data and analytics iteration process alive.

In the next two chapters, we will delve more deeply into some of the foundational requirements and conditions that set the stage for analytics transformation: the setting of meaningful organizational goals and D&A strategy, and the roles, expertise and organizational culture attributes needed to link business and analytics in a shared mission.

To Summarize:

Analytics Fitness is a sequence of five stages that represent an organization's readiness and ability to make informed business decisions through the effective use of data. With each successive stage comes improved technological capabilities and infrastructure, greater analytics expertise, a clearer D&A strategy, and increased alignment between business and analytics teams. As organizations advance through the higher Analytics Fitness levels, their analytics sophistication and increasingly open and democratic data culture become mutually reinforcing. Greater communication, transparency and data access fuels further innovation and analytics sophistication. Each step on the Analytics Fitness ladder can be viewed as a milestone in the organization's analytics and digital transformation journey. The ultimate goal of Analytics Fitness is to bring an organization closer to adopting the *Data as a Horizontal* paradigm.

Essential Takeaways:

- *Analytics engineering* refers to an AI end-to-end process involving business problem framing, data preparation, model building, automation, and embedded analytics
- A UAP will allow for data self-serviceability, democratization, promotion of data discovery, and exploration to move the organization closer to the *Data as a Horizontal* paradigm.
- Single source of truth (SSOT) is primarily a guideline that encourages all employees to use the same data.

- Organizations that use the Analytics Fitness framework as milestones and follow its sequence of stages will move closer to the *Data as a Horizontal* paradigm: the ultimate goal of Analytics Fitness.
- Analytics Fitness Level I is the entry point in the analytics fitness framework. At this stage, organizations are heavily reliant on spreadsheets and make critical decisions based on siloed data, resulting in "multiple versions of the truth" to explain what happened in the past.[28]
- In Analytics Fitness Levels II and III, organizations use descriptive analytics to identify a small number of "high-leverage" business problems that are tightly defined, can be addressed promptly, and are likely to produce evident business value, and then focus on those to show business results.
- To reach Analytics Fitness Levels IV and V, organizations need to invest heavily in Big Data technologies and build a robust UAP. They must also hire talented, high-performing individuals with experience in very specialized areas of advanced analytics, an entrepreneurial spirit, and superior problem-solving skills.

---

28   https://staywell.mydigitalpublication.com/publication/?m=23234&i=735023&view=articleBrowser&article_id=4194920&ver=html5

Chapter 4

The Analytics Triad™: Goals, Metrics, and Data & Analytics Strategy

In Chapter 2 (*Why Link Analytics and Business?*), we discussed the many benefits organizations can reap when they become data-driven, promote the widespread accessibility of institutional data (Data as a Horizontal), and achieve what we refer to as Analytics Fitness. And, in Chapter 3 (*Analytics Fitness™*), we examined the levels of analytics readiness that constitute each stage in the journey toward analytics transformation (*Fig. 18*).

Fig. 18: Converting raw data to actionable insights

Now it is time to look more closely at organizational goal setting and the framing of a sound data and analytics (D&A) strategy, without which the analytics engineering process cannot successfully get off the ground. Familiarity with the terms introduced in this chapter will facilitate fruitful discussion with program managers, product managers, and executives in your group.

The Analytics Triad

Data that is to form the basis for an analytics project must be collected and analyzed according to a cohesive strategy that is informed by the organization's overarching business goals and the framing of specific business problems. According to McKinsey, only 30 percent of organizations align their analytics strategy with their broader corporate strategy.[29] Analytics projects are only useful if they are directed to answering meaningful business questions or resolving organizational challenges identified as priorities by management. A data-driven culture starts at the very top.

Businesses that ignore the need for clear organizational goals and a cohesive D&A strategy will find their analytics efforts confined to tactical issues and will continue to reside at the lower end of the Analytics Fitness scale. Analytics digital transformation can be successful only if there is alignment on organizational goals, strategy and metrics, a constellation of factors that we will refer to as The Analytics Triad (*Fig. 19*).

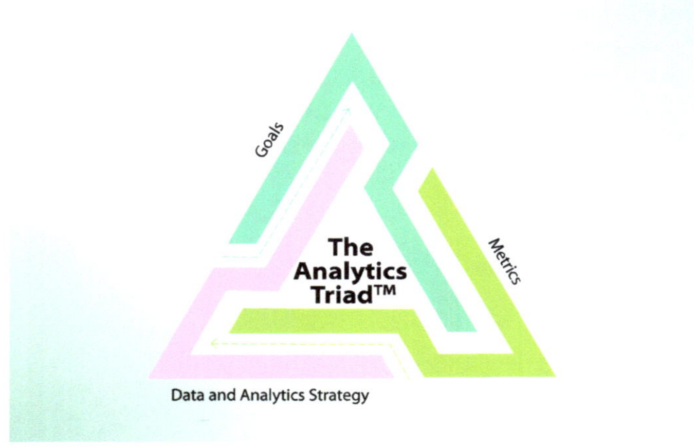

Fig. 19: The Analytics Triad

Organizational Goals and Objectives

Organizational goals are powerful energizers that conceptualize and articulate the future direction of an organization. They can motivate employees to take shared ownership of projects and facilitate the alignment of individual and team efforts. A goal is a statement that elucidates a future desired state that an organization strives to reach. These statements can be strategic, painting long-term objectives in broad brush strokes. Objectives, on the other hand, are tactical, drilling deeper to focus on short-term operational endeavors within discrete business units.

In the previous chapters, we touched on the ways in which the growing pervasiveness of data over the past several decades has changed not only the way organizations function but also the way they think. Decades have now elapsed since the genesis of descriptive analytics, which helped popularize the notion that business decisions should be based on data and facts, rather than intuition alone. In that time, the setting of objectives and the quantitative

---

29   https://www.mckinsey.com/capabilities/quantumblack/our-insights/accelerating-analytics-to-navigate-covid-19-and-the-next-normal

measurement of organizational progress toward meeting them have become de rigueur. There are now very few businesses that don't focus on metrics, the concrete units into which objectives are broken down for the purpose of tracking progress.

Metrics, KPIs and OKRs

A business metric can be used to measure an individual or group's performance toward meeting set objectives that, collectively, line up to fulfill an organization's overarching goals. Goals are generally long-term (three to five years), providing vision and a general organizational orientation.[30] Objectives are concrete implementation steps or deliverables that an organization pursues to reach its goals. They lay out concrete parameters such as *Who? When? What? Where?*

In the 1980s, a system of metric-validated performance evaluation was established by corporate consultant George Doran that became the favored method for setting organizational objectives through that decade and beyond. Doran introduced the "SMART" acronym (which dictated that objectives should be Specific, Measurable, Achievable, Relevant, and Time-bound). His system was formulated to address concerns that business objectives were often too vague and diffuse to bring about concrete results. By the 1990s, a new term, key performance indicators (KPIs), was introduced to describe metrics targeted to reaching a predetermined objective. If mapped well, KPIs provide a scorecard of past organizational performance that can be used to predict future challenges and return on investment (ROI).[31] *(Fig. 20)*

Fig. 20: Key components of metrics or KPI

---

30   https://www.michigan.gov/documents/8-pub207_60743_7.pdf

31   https://hbr.org/2021/09/kpis-arent-just-about-assessing-past-performance?utm_campaign=hbr&utm_medium=social&utm_source=linkedin

Yet another business management schema, objectives and key results (OKRs), is now gaining traction in the technology sector. Initially introduced by Intel in the 1970's, OKRs are emerging as the go-to method top tech companies are using to measure success.[32] Andy Grove, in 1995, published a management manual, *High Output Management*, where he popularized the concept of OKRs, which help organizations focus on a set of priorities that will help them reach a desired state (*Fig. 21*).

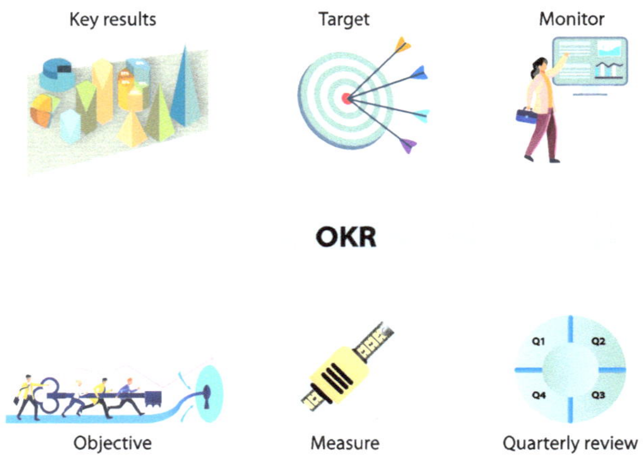

Fig. 21: Key components of OKRs (objectives and key results)

Where KPIs are focused on measuring and highlighting how a business unit is performing against its objectives, OKRs establish objectives and then measure and monitor deliverables that lead to the broader fulfillment of an organization's goals. The following are two key questions to consider when outlining OKRs:

- *Where do I want to go?* (desired state, north star, beacon)
- *How will I know I'm getting there?* (measurement and monitoring)

Chosen prudently, metrics—whether set out as KPIs or OKRs—are a quantifiable measure that can be used to evaluate and keep track of the success or failure of components of a business. Metrics can reveal overall performance inefficiencies, jumpstart operational excellence, continue sustainable growth, and help organizations remain competitive in the marketplace.

While some metrics are easy to measure, others may be elusive and challenging to identify, measure, and monitor. In such cases, researching organizational, operational process maps; identifying decision areas; and garnering inputs from various executive heads and subject matter experts (SMEs) are steps that can be taken to design the elusive metric.

---

32   https://blog.weekdone.com/what-companies-use-okrs/

Metrics can be used to measure, monitor, and chart progress across every functional area of a business. In sales verticals, for example, metrics can measure overall sales strategy, market penetration, individual sales processes, and pipelines. Further, they can be used to adjust employee compensation, commissions, and bonuses, and prepare for a growth trajectory. If sales operation managers, chief financial officers, and analysts judiciously monitor sales metrics through scrupulous tracking and measurement, for example, they can catch bottlenecks and make timely adjustments to their sales initiatives.

A combination of lagging and leading indicators can be measured to gain a view of an organization's current state and the challenges and opportunities that can determine its future. Lagging indicators, including the following, can be captured using the descriptive analytics we reviewed in Chapter 2 (*Why Link Analytics to Business?*):

- Customer attrition
- Loss of revenue
- Market penetration percentage
- Contracts, leads per period
- Revenue, sales by product, region
- Customer lifetime value
- Conversion rate (measured by team, individual, or location)
- Sales funnel components

Predictive and prescriptive analytics, by contrast, can be used to monitor leading indicators and forward-looking metrics, such as the following:

- Sales forecasting
- Pipeline opportunities
- Opportunity conversion
- Team and sales representative closing ratio by product and region
- Customer visits

Setting a Data and Analytics (D&A) Strategy

A D&A strategy is an evolving blueprint that outlines what data organizations should collect, maintain, and analyze to incorporate analytics and data-driven decision-making into organizational practice. A D&A strategy is a necessity for any organization that wishes to leverage data as a strategic asset and gain a competitive advantage in the marketplace. To execute a D&A strategy, a business will draw on its organizational analytics capabilities, management systems, and resources.

D&A strategy not only determines what data to collect but also how it is to be analyzed. For example, let us say an organization has created specific, measurable, attainable, relevant, time-bound goals to boost revenue, reduce cost, augment process efficiencies, and incorporate technological advancements. It plans to reach its goals and gain a competitive advantage using information and data-driven decision-making and requires its analytics function to support both management consultant–type projects and innovative data products. To meet its goals, it will need to develop a D&A strategy that goes beyond familiar data reporting and descriptive analytics efforts to harness the power of advanced analytics.

Some of the typical questions raised in the process of defining an organization's D&A strategy include the following:

- What are our overarching organizational goals and what insights will we require/ questions will we need to answer to meet those goals?
- What are the specific business problem statements that will dictate our D&A strategy?
- What kinds of data should we collect, why do we need it (business rationalization), and what benefits will it bring (business outcomes)?
- From where (and how) do we plan to obtain the data that will form the basis for our analytics efforts: from internal sources, external sources, or both?
- How do we plan to store the data and make it available in a format that can be used by our analytics models? What are the technical capabilities we will need (such as a UAP) to collect, manage and analyze our data?
- What level of analytics sophistication (descriptive, predictive or prescriptive) will be required of the analytics models we plan to use?

The consequences of failing to resolve such questions and lay out a clear D&A roadmap can be expensive, resulting in a succession of failed analytics projects or costly efforts to repair the holes left by an inadequate D&A strategy. Some organizations, for example, may be forced to invest heavily in data management and data governance systems to untangle the complex web of data stored in separate department silos. Others may have to bring in analytics consultants, Big Data architects and other experts to reconcile, rationalize, validate, and verify the data they have amassed with no clear strategy or purpose.

Many businesses make the mistake of opting for hackathon analytics, undermining their analytics projects with a mad dash to the finish line, resulting in outcomes that are not scalable or repeatable. And some engage in shotgun analytics, pursuing analytics efforts with no clear strategy, theory, or justification, just to "see what sticks."

Of course, forging an enterprise D&A strategy is no easy task. Legacy organizations with mounting technical debt and a lack of previous investment in digital transformation initiatives are likely to face particular challenges. In these organizations, data discovery and D&A strategy-setting is often thwarted by artificial internal data boundaries and silos that reduce transparency around existing business operations and functions. These silos may derive from a reluctance to share information, a thinly veiled effort to avoid relinquishing power. In such cases, disparate groups may have come up with their own data collection parameters, semantics, and vernacular, or may have implemented their own makeshift data validation and verification processes or data literacy efforts.

These siloed endeavors will result in confusion when D&A projects generated in individual business verticals are viewed from an enterprise standpoint. This fragmentation can prevent an organization from gaining a holistic view of the state of its business, making it next to impossible to answer simple questions such as, "How are we doing now?" and "What steps do we need to take to reach our goals?" It can also result in misplaced expectations concerning data pipelines, updates, maintenance schedules, archiving, and data quality.

In organizations plagued by lack of a data strategy or shared D&A vernacular, information consumers and IT professionals are likely to find themselves communicating at cross purposes. Managers and others who have not done the foundational work of framing clear business questions or attaining a functional level of data literacy can find themselves stuck in a cyclical loop with the organization's information providers, a futile push and pull that leads to frustration and loss of productivity.

To illustrate the critical importance of thoughtful problem framing, and D&A strategy-setting, let us consider the hypothetical situation of a manager at an organization that is still at the beginning of its D&A journey:

KK & Sons Case Study

The Data

Imagine that you are the manager responsible for diversity and inclusion (D&I) and accessibility initiatives for KK & Sons. Your executive team has not issued a specific, measurable, attainable, trackable (SMART) and time-bound goal; instead, what they have shared with you is, "*Let us get better at D&I.*" You create an ad hoc data report and plot the global employee headcount by gender over the years. There is room for improvement, as always, but the trends *are* pointing in the right direction. Time to put the green checkmark next to the D&I goals for the quarter.

The Analysis

Since you are delighted with your accomplishment in the D&I analysis, you share the results with an engineering manager, your friend from college, while waiting in line to get a cappuccino. After a long pause, she gives her signature sigh. "Truly, the numbers you are trying to declare victory with are not right," she says in a quavering voice. She is the only woman senior engineering manager in the organization and starts counting on just one hand the number of female engineers that have made it past the senior software engineer level to either leadership or the architect track on her floor. She shares with you more examples of inequities in the workplace.

She then makes a suggestion: to break down employee headcount by gender, geography, engineering vs. non-engineering roles, compensation, pay equity, promotions, work history, manager training, employee training, conference attendance, support, mentorship, and sponsorship programs.

Unfortunately, there is no one system—a UAP—to pull all the information you need. For example, employee compensation is in a separate HR (Human Resources) system, and you don't have access to this confidential information. Your work has suddenly become a bit difficult, but you are committed to finding the answers you need, and your friend offers to help with the data access and analysis.

Insights and Preliminary Results

You embark on exploratory data analysis (EDA), redo the graphs, and drill down on some of the specifics your friend suggested. You uncover valuable new insights that may have been missed if you hadn't combined two data sources and analyzed them together. Now you find that there are certain business pockets within engineering that are not doing so well at D&I. You now have *actionable, usable, obtainable* information you can draw upon to refine your focus in the next quarter. You now have measurable objectives based on metrics, not just vague goals. Technical hiring, pay equity, promotions, and diversity in middle management and upper management are all areas in which you can use analytics to bring about advancements.

Imagine how much simpler your task would have been from the outset if you had been given the same task in a data-driven organization that assigned SMART objectives and was equipped with a UAP. And think about how much easier still it would have been in a less siloed business that was committed to data transparency and the close integration of its business and analytics teams.

Who Sets D&A Strategy?

Identifying the right business metrics to measure, tracking and monitoring them against a goal, and mapping the dynamic relationships between KPIs themselves should be a collaborative undertaking for the analytics team, executives, and subject matter experts (SMEs) across an organization. According to a 2020 article published by Joe Shapiro in the *Harvard Business Review*, while the high-level objectives of an advanced analytics project must be set by management, project scoping can only be done by an organization's advanced analytics team:

"Communication around what is reasonable and deliverable given current capabilities must come from the data scientists—not the frontline marketing person in an agency or the business unit leader."[33]

Shapiro further goes on to say that complete alignment between team business and team advanced analytics is required for project success.[67] Management expectations must be aligned with the organization's data science capabilities and realistic delivery estimates.

Business leaders and data scientists should jointly decide which business problems to focus on.[34] Indeed, framing a business problem and achieving alignment on D&A strategy are the first two steps in the analytics engineering process that we outlined in Chapter 3 (*Analytics Fitness*).

---

33   https://hbr.org/2020/02/are-your-companys-leaders-and-data-scientists-on-the-same-page
34   https://hbr.org/2020/03/whats-the-best-approach-to-data-analytics

Forging a Data Collection Plan

Data Discovery

Once a business problem has been identified and framed, the organization will need to determine what data it will need to collect to shed light on that problem. Team business and team analytics must also agree on the analytics methodology and degree of sophistication that will be needed to deliver pertinent insights and generate value (*Fig. 22*). Whether the organization intends to employ descriptive analytics or to embark upon a more sophisticated endeavor using predictive or prescriptive analytics models, it will begin in the same place. Indeed, the purpose of data collection has not been significantly reconceptualized since spreadsheets and relational databases were first introduced.

Fig. 22: Generating value from data

Identifying what to collect and how much to collect should be a collaborative decision made by analytics team members, engineers, domain experts, and user representatives. Consideration should be given to technical nuances, business challenges, the organization's current stage of technological evolution, and desired output.

First, the organization will need to take inventory of the data that is already available and determine how that data fits into its overarching data strategy. It may well be that leveraging existing data, whether it sits in a data silo or has been gathered by a more centralized group, will be enough to generate valuable insights into the business problem it seeks to address.

Companies with a dysfunctional organizational culture may find that accessing data that exists in their internal silos can be more strenuous than initiating new data collection efforts. The executives who "own" the sought-after data may resist doing the "extra work" of managing the extract, transform, load (ETL) jobs (to be discussed in greater detail in Chapter 6) that pull and package the required data. The "extra work" excuse is typically mobilized to provide cover for a political and organizational reluctance to share information or an unwillingness to work collaboratively towards an organization's goals. While it may seem a logical, practical, time- and cost-saving endeavor to harvest and share existing data instead of reinventing the wheel, organizations lacking effective leadership and a healthy internal culture do not always choose this course.

The need to prevail upon colleagues in various business verticals to manually pull the relevant data is further complicated by a lack of data standardization across an organization. Something as simple as an employee's name, which should be used in a consistent way across business verticals, may be stored with different permutations in different functional silos. This means that precious data may be obscured by conflicting information. Making matters worse, software applications and dashboards may have been built on top of the disparate databases used within business silos. In such cases, it will be more difficult to untangle the lineage of the data and the data context in which it was derived. Retrieving data context or metric definitions during data discovery may not be possible without the advice of a person who has tribal knowledge of the data in question. Knowledge may need to be extracted from prior data users, architects, engineers, or those who created the data pipelines. These efforts can be time-consuming and challenging, especially in organizations that lack a culture of transparency and collaboration.

The Significance of a UAP

Each of the challenges described above would be obviated by the existence of a UAP, which enables analytics practitioners to pull in data seamlessly and reconcile it for use in analytics models. A UAP creates connections between siloed data, enabling organizations to innovate rapidly.[35] Organizations typically add the building of a UAP to their strategic goals, as it takes time to construct a strong data foundation and robust data processing systems and pipelines.

Managing and Scoping New Data Collection Efforts

In cases where organizational data has not been sufficiently amassed or is otherwise unavailable, a company may have to initiate new internal data collection efforts. Such efforts must be carefully managed by the cross-functional project team—composed of business executives, analytics practitioners, and subject matter experts, as discussed above—so that considerations around scope, purpose and cost are balanced appropriately.

Data collection can be initiated in various ways: through surveys, interviews, hiring third-party vendors, conducting web searches, or gathering organizational data from internal systems. (*Fig. 23*).

---

35   https://databricks.com/glossary/unified-data-analytics-platform

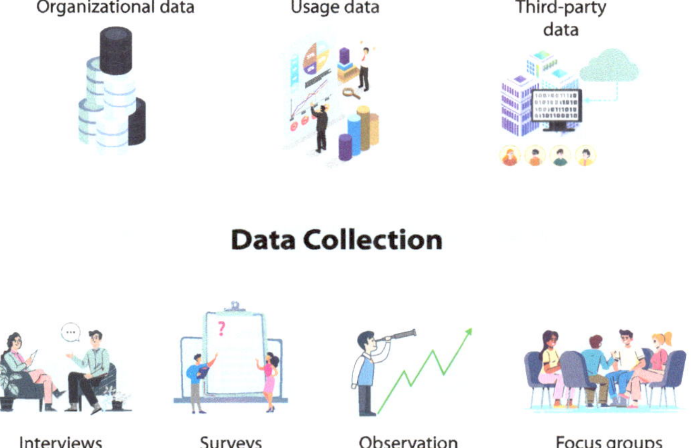

Fig. 23: Methods of data collection

Project teams often run into thorny issues and disagreements over how much data to collect. These disputes can be fueled by both legitimate considerations and unproductive factors involving organizational politics and internal culture.

When you initiate data collection, you may have only one shot at collecting it. The more data you collect, the higher the chance of finding patterns, associations, and relationships within it. For this reason, tech-savvy companies—buoyed by advances in Big Data technologies and low compute and storage costs—are adopting a *"collect everything"* mantra.

Leaders of organizations on the lower rungs of the Analytics Fitness ladder may be swayed by reports from top business schools, marketing blogs, and top-dollar consultants trumpeting the success stories of top-tier tech companies that have implemented gargantuan D&A projects. They may likewise seek to cast their own data collection net wide, burdening their analytics teams with requests and pressure to collect more data than they need. In IT-centric organizations that have legacy systems and limited budgets, however, data collection projects that are initiated with a *"just in case"* or *"store it and it will come"* rationale can be a drain on scarce resources.

Building a data collection pipeline requires skilled data engineers, data architects, and data development operational engineers (Data DevOps) to build, process, clean, and maintain the pipeline. Assembling such expertise can be a costly proposition (*Fig. 24*). Commercial cloud platforms such as Azure, AWS, Teradata, Databricks, and Snowflake are helping to reduce the cost of analytics infrastructure, but processing and distilling high-quality data still comes at a price.

Fig. 24: Development operations (DevOps)

Runaway data collection undertaken by organizations with little experience and a haphazard D&A strategy also raises other problems. Companies that amass data without a coherent plan may risk falling foul of legal data policies and compliance related to privacy. A constellation of state, federal and international data protection regulations exist to protect consumers from having their personal information fall into the wrong hands. The CCPA (California Consumer Privacy Act), SOX (the Sarbanes-Oxley Act of 2002), and GDPR (Europe's General Data Protection Regulation) are just a few of the regulations that are enforced by state attorneys general, government agencies, and self-regulatory organizations. Privacy regulations must always be factored in when data collection is initiated. These regulations are the province of qualified data governance professionals who should be a fixture in all companies that handle data—essentially all companies in today's business landscape. (The personnel needed for a robust data governance infrastructure will be discussed in Chapter 5).

Striking the right balance between the costs and benefits of casting a wide net vs. carefully scoping data collection efforts is vital and will depend on each business's unique circumstances. Organizations must consider their budgets, technical talent, organizational culture, and the availability of skilled human capital.

While tech-savvy companies with a flourishing data culture are equipped to take advantage of torrents of Big Data, legacy companies just beginning their analytics journey are well advised to prudently align their data collection efforts with tailored organizational goals and business problem statements. For such organizations, a tempered, thoughtful, and iterative approach to data collection will also enable them to harness actionable results instead of being sidetracked by hasty conclusions generated by incomplete, inaccurate, or irrelevant data.

It may be beneficial for the project team, working closely with an executive sponsor, to break down the question of "*What to collect?*" into short-term and long-term goals (*Fig. 25*). This is especially the case when projects are burdened with constrained resources, competing priorities, unexpected delays, and unforeseen challenges. Under these circumstances, project teams will be forced to break their data collection goals into smaller pieces and refine their efforts slowly. However, they should not lose sight of the fundamental purpose of their data collection efforts. They should remain mindful of why the organization needs the data they are gathering (business rationalization) and what benefits the data is expected to bring (business outcomes).

Fig. 25: What to collect?

External data is a source that is often overlooked in the data collection design and planning phase. Depending on the nature of the business problem to be solved, the assimilation of external data may be very valuable. Marketing and advertising data can be purchased, while government data is typically accessible free of charge. Blending external data with internal organizational data can yield golden nuggets of information that can help refine the goals and scope of descriptive and advanced analytics projects, enrich corporate perceptiveness, and enhance the analytical value chain.

In essence, blending a variety of data sources (internal or external) and performing exploratory data analysis (EDA) when building advanced analytics models increases the chances that the project will unearth hidden relationships, patterns, and insights. This benefit is especially important in complex advanced analytics projects, where the type of data sought is comparatively abstract and nebulous in the early stages of the discovery phase. The kinds of issues EDA is capable of uncovering are wide-ranging. They may include patterns of unexpected top customer and revenue loss, multiple product returns, or complaints of poor customer service in a specific location, loss of market share, manufacturing part failures, or any of a vast array of other issues.

In addition to the questions laid out previously in this chapter, the following essentials must also be considered before initiating data collection:

- What data type, format and granularity will best fit our goals?
- What topics or metrics should be included?
- How will we structure our collected data and establish relationships between them?
- How will we store our data to make it available for use in our analytics models?

Data Type

The data that an organization collects, whether internal or external, can take two main forms: structured and unstructured. Which of the two data types an organization chooses to collect—structured, unstructured, or both—will have a profound impact on the rest of its D&A strategy. This decision will affect everything from the data storage and management solutions that will be needed to house and retrieve the data to the sophistication of the models that can be used to analyze that data.

Structured Data

Structured data is predefined, formatted data, also referred to as *transactional data* because it consists of records (*transactions*). It is organized in a *table* format with rows (records) and columns (fields) and kept in a *relational database*. A relational database is an organized collection of structured data, which is in turn managed by a relational database management system (RDBMS). Structured data possesses the lowest level of complexity and sophistication in the data taxonomy and is considered entry-level.

The figure below shows an example of a database containing structured data stored in multiple tables *(Fig. 26)*.

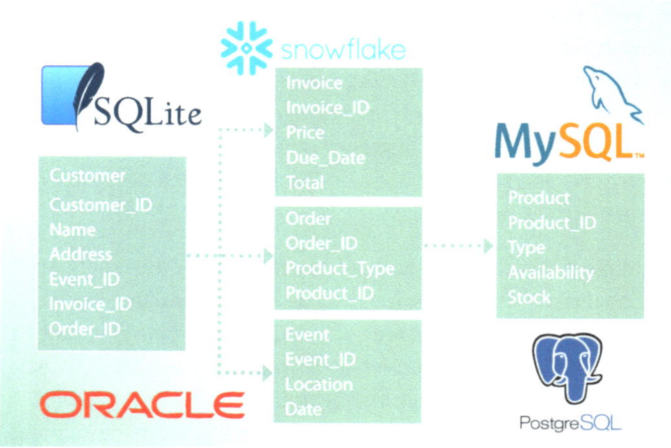

Fig. 26: Illustration of a database with transactional data

Customer information, banking transactions, contracts, invoices, and stock information are examples of structured data, often compiled in CSV files and simple spreadsheets. Structured data is used heavily in most organizations. There are many tools and technologies designed to manage structured data, and employees have decades of experience handling it.

The figure below (*Fig. 27*) represents a typical example of structured data, in this case showing customer purchase transaction and order-related information. The fields in database table columns can hold different data types, such as numbers, hyperlinks, and text.

Order_ID	Order_Type	Product_ID	Product_Locaction	Address_ID
Order1	OrderType1	Product1	Location1	Address1
Order2	OrderType1	Product2	Location2	Address2

Fig. 27: Representation of structured customer purchase transactional data

The figure below *(Fig. 28)* represents an event table in the same relational database as the example above.

Event_ID	Location	Date
Event1	Location1	Date1
Event2	Location2	Date2

Fig. 28: Event table in a relational database with transactional data

Structured data, residing at the lowest level of the data taxonomy, is primarily used for descriptive analytics.

Despite the limitations of structured data, businesses have made great strides mobilizing the power of descriptive analytics.[36] In the last decade, businesses that have been primarily focused on using structured data have pivoted from the world of spreadsheets to *business process management (BPM)* and *business process improvement (BPI)* tools. BPM tools permit organizations to keep track of business-related activities and enhance their operational excellence. Examples of functions managed by BPM tools include departmental workflows, handoffs, sign-offs, and the maintenance of contracts, invoices, and customer information. BPM tools have access to organized sets of *structured data* stored in a computer *database*. They are often referred to as *BI*, or *"business intelligence,"* tools.

The following are a few examples specific business domains in which BI tools are used:

- Customer or potential customer tracking and customer relationship management (CRM) for sales and marketing life cycles

---

36   https://www.enterpriseappstoday.com/stats/business-intelligence-statistics.html

- Supply chain management (SCM) for inventory management
- Electronic health records (EHR) for patient records
- Clinical decision support systems (CDSS) for drug trials

BI tools have pre-built templates, developed with industry-specific terminology, rule sets, practices, workflows, and scenarios by which underlying business records are reviewed and relationships found between the various types of information stored in databases.

New-generation BI tools equip managers with a presentation layer that enables them to derive valuable insights from data without requiring them to have any particular technical knowledge. Through dashboards, users can access meaningful data without needing to know anything about the underlying architecture, the storage system, or even the inner workings of the business rule sets and principles used to compile the data.

Managers no longer need to track down the mysterious unicorn team or wizard engineer to fold business records into relational databases or introduce business logic into organic systems to reduce repetitive, time-consuming, error-prone, and manual tasks. They can now buy off-the-shelf solutions that cover 80% of their use cases. Front-line workers can now use tools embedded with simple analytics to perform assigned tasks effectively, thereby improving productivity and employee morale.

These advances are partly due to the accessibility of handy and inexpensive commercial "software as a service" solutions, decades of established expertise in creating management reports, worker experience handling structured data, and the availability of established data warehouse technologies.

There is, however, a yawning gap between the capabilities of descriptive analytics/ BI and the insights that can be generated by its advanced analytics cousins, predictive and prescriptive analytics. Whereas descriptive analytics/BI focuses on the analysis of structured data, advanced analytics mines valuable information from the analysis of unstructured data.

Unstructured Data

We live in the information age, in which we are no longer just the consumers of technology but also its products. In the interconnected data ecosystem known as the Internet of Things (IoT), we generate a vast amount of data from a tremendous array of sources. We generate sensor data from our health apps, unknowingly share our location and other personal information while streaming music on our phones or viewing social media posts and photos. We create digital exhaust as we use the internet. We are also routinely surveilled by security cameras as we make our way from home to the bank or the corner delicatessen (*Fig. 29*).

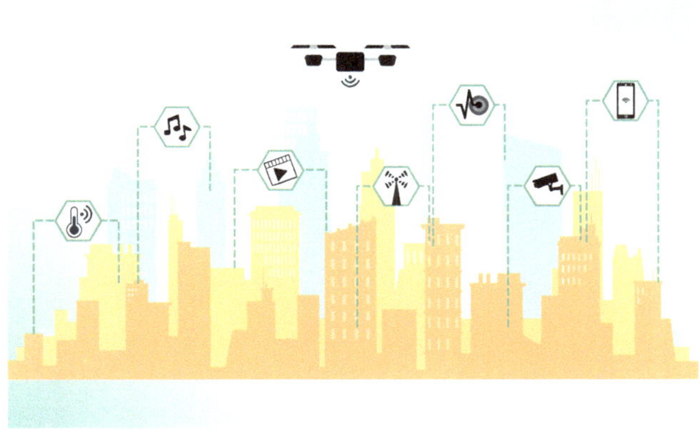

Fig. 29: Devices generating various data streams

The items (objects, files) generated from these sources, which can range from a few bytes to terabytes in size, are known as *unstructured data*. Unstructured data is not organized in a predefined, searchable format like structured data, which follows a conventional data model and fits neatly into a database.

Unstructured data can include media and entertainment data, surveillance data, geospatial data, weather data, sensor data, stock ticker data, emails, productivity applications, document collections, and invoices. Whether we like it or not, we are consumers and generators of unstructured data.

The figure below summarizes the key differences between structured and unstructured data *(Fig. 30)*.[37]

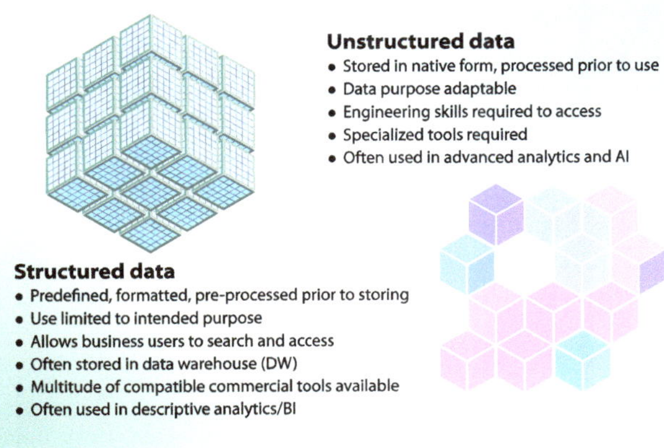

Fig. 30: Structured and unstructured data comparison

---

37   https://www.talend.com/resources/structured-vs-unstructured-data/

The engineers involved in algorithm development in advanced analytics projects will typically use raw, unstructured data, instead of summarized or processed data, to write analytics software to find patterns and hidden relationships. In advanced analytics algorithms and modeling, unprocessed data provides inputs that will yield new values to solve business problems. The results of the algorithms and models will then be stored in relational databases for descriptive analytics. Organizations should thus give sufficient thought to architect-appropriate solutions for both descriptive and advanced analytics workloads.

Businesses today are under pressure to leverage all types of data and various analytics categories. Organizations that are limited to default approaches that use only structured data, descriptive analytics, and BI reporting are likely to find themselves on the back foot. Agile, data-driven businesses are using sophisticated ML, statistical methods, and mathematical and operations research techniques to take advantage of their troves of raw data.

Considering Data Storage

Decisions about the type (structured or unstructured), source, and quantity of data to be collected for analytics engineering projects are inextricably connected to the issue of data storage, as the two have a symbiotic relationship. Neither data collection nor data storage happens in isolation, and consideration of one should always include an assessment of its impact on the other. D&A strategy must address the optimization of both if an organization's data is to be made available in the appropriate form for use in its analytics endeavors.

To enable the widespread adoption of the data collected by an organization, it must be in the right format for each internal audience to consume. Hence, careful consideration must be given to choosing a storage method that will make data available to the right user population in the right form. For instance, unstructured or "raw" data may be too granular, have too much information, and produce poor results when queried by users without sophisticated analytics skill sets. Raw, unstructured data in its native form may also be incompatible with an organization's existing analytics software or the current tools available in the enterprise toolbox.

Businesses that are limited to storing their data in traditional relational databases face severe constraints, as these databases can only store structured data. Relational databases require a schema (rows, columns, tables, and relationships in the database) and a predefined data format (schema on write) before writing into the database.

Organizations that must rely on relational databases and first-generation enterprise data warehouses (EDWs) also face other challenges and limitations. Relational databases and EDWs fall into the category of traditional, centralized, monolithic data infrastructure, where one business vertical, typically IT (information technology), manages all the organizational data.[38] These platforms are tied to specific data technologies and maintained

---

38   https://www.softlanding.ca/blog/data-mesh-a-fresh-approach-to-data-organization/

and driven by hyper-specialized (and centralized) engineers. The engineers in the business vertical control all data ingestion and pipeline and transformation efforts.

EDWs support only a limited set of specialized business users. Most analytics efforts in organizations dependent upon EDWs are limited to BI or descriptive analytics and their organizational data is typically underutilized. Ultimately, businesses using EDWs are not able to realize the full benefit of their data as a strategic asset.

New data management technologies are being invented to overcome the challenges and limitations associated with relational databases. Big Data implementations are capitalizing on the improvements in the performance of hardware, CPU and memory, and their continued reduction in cost. These updated hardware technologies are implemented using relatively inexpensive commodity services and offer multiple cores, hundreds of gigabytes of memory, and multiprocessing for speed and agility.

Facing a future characterized by rapidly changing market demands, expanding technology footprints, and continual technology advancement, businesses of every size and sector are accelerating their move to the cloud to enhance the speed, agility, security, and value of their IT investments.[39] Cloud computing is a viable alternative to hardware, and one that is cheaper up-front, as well as in overall CAPEX (capital expenditure).

In the evolving digital age, the case for transitioning to modern cloud solutions—including software-as-a-service (SaaS), public and private clouds platforms, and data centers—has never been clearer.

According to a 2022 Technology Survey published by KPMG:[40]

- 75 percent of survey participants said their organizations are currently migrating their strategic workloads to the cloud
- 14 percent have completed migration and are now looking to optimize
- 30 percent of organizations surveyed have migrated more than 60 percent of their enterprise workloads to the cloud

The latest technological advances offered by Amazon Web Services (AWS), Simple Storage Service (S3), Microsoft Azure, Tera Data, Databricks, and other on-demand cloud data solutions have precluded the need for vast, long-term infrastructure investments.

Cloud computing analytics platforms use file systems or object stores that do not care what you write to the platform and can be loaded without any preprocessing. With these platforms, the schema is created only while reading the data (schema on read). This option yields flexibility, query power, and the ability to bring in new data sources on the fly.

---

39   https://info.kpmg.us/news-perspectives/technology-innovation/kpmg-2022-technology-survey.html
40   See note 39 above.

Organizations can now pivot from the strained capabilities of traditional relational databases to distributed computing that provides efficient support for flexible and variable data constructs without compromising data integrity. Data stored in a relational database can be accessed only by that relational database. Big Data platforms, by contrast, are modular. They are designed to access the same file using various tools and technologies. Current technologies such as Hive and Spark use SQL-like queries to access data. Adopting Big Data technologies will allow organizations to weather major technological and cultural shifts.

In Chapter 6 (*Managing Data for Transformational Analytics*), we will take a closer look at the evolution of data storage and management solutions and the spectrum of new technology platforms now available to handle these functions. First, however, we must take a closer look at the human factors that play into analytics initiatives. In Chapter 5 (*Linking Analytics to Business: Roles, Expertise and Organizational Culture*), we will discuss the core team members and expertise that should be in place if an organization is to optimize its analytics efforts. We will also continue to examine the role organizational culture can play in fueling analytics success or derailing an organization's analytics transformation.

To Summarize:

Analytics projects must be guided by a cohesive D&A strategy that is in alignment with an organization's overarching goals. Analytics efforts launched without strategic forethought are likely to be of limited usefulness, if they can be accomplished at all. D&A strategy setting should be a collaborative effort that involves business leaders, subject matter experts, and members of the organization's analytics team.

D&A strategy should focus on both large-order issues and more granular ones. It should be tailored to address well-formulated business problem statements and answer fundamental questions that will facilitate decision-making by leadership. It should also provide a roadmap for the analytics project team, determining what data should be collected, how it should be stored and managed, and what analytics methodology should be used to analyze it.

The answers to these questions will depend on the organization's current level of Analytics Fitness, its D&A budget, the extent of management support for the analytics project, and many other factors unique to each business at the time a project is launched. D&A strategy must factor in a range of practical considerations. An organization's data storage capabilities, for example, will bear upon what data it is able to collect and the type of analysis it is able to use.

A company's culture and mode of organization will affect the scope and course of any analytics project it takes on. Siloed and dysfunctional organizations will face more challenges than those that have cultivated a culture of transparency and collaboration.

Essential Takeaways:

- Goals describe the future state an organization will strive to reach. They are generally long term (three to five years) and provide vision and direction.[41]
- Objectives are concrete implementation steps or deliverables an organization works to accomplish on the way to reaching its overarching goals. They specify who, what, when, and where, and they are often measured quantitatively, in the form of metrics.
- KPIs (key performance indicators) and OKRs (objectives and key results) are two methods that have emerged to measure an organization's progress toward meeting its goals.
- An organization's goals and objectives should play a central role in D&A strategy setting.
- D&A strategy sets a roadmap for the data that is to be collected and how that data will be processed, stored, managed, and analyzed in order to facilitate fact-based decision-making.
- The purpose of data collection is to generate insights and value from the gathered data.
- Before a data collection strategy is established, data discovery should be conducted to take inventory of the type and amount of data the organization already possesses, how it is stored, and whether and how it can be accessed for use in the current analytics project.
- If new data is to be collected, D&A strategy must consider its type, format, granularity, and storage requirements.
- Structured and unstructured data are the two major data types. Structured data is organized in a table format, stored in relational databases, and used for descriptive analytics or BI. Unstructured data does not have a prewritten format and can take a wide variety of forms. Unstructured data is used in advanced analytics to uncover hidden patterns and relationships and to yield new values to solve business problems.
- Using only structured data will confine an organization to descriptive analytics, the lowest level in the analytics hierarchy, as predictive and prescriptive analytics require unstructured data.
- Unstructured data cannot be stored in traditional relational databases and requires the use of newer data management technologies.
- Advances in Big Data and cloud computing are reducing the cost and increasing the accessibility of more flexible, modular data storage and management solutions.

---

41   https://www.michigan.gov/documents/8-pub207_60743_7.pdf

Chapter 5

Linking Analytics to Business: Roles, Expertise, and Organizational Culture

As we have established, setting a sound D&A strategy requires a sophisticated, multi-functional team that includes representatives from company management and an organization's analytics team. Because D&A strategy marries business thinking with an engineer's understanding of data collection and management techniques, sophisticated modeling capabilities, and technical operationalization, this amalgamation of skills is essential for project success. *(Fig. 31)*

Fig. 31: Linking analytics and business

While this merger of expertise makes perfect sense in the abstract, however, maintaining a smoothly functioning analytics project team with the appropriate authority and know-how can be a challenge when that team is composed of flesh-and-blood people.

Analytics and Business: Different Planets or Different Universes?

It is an unfortunate fact that, in mainstream and non–technology-focused organizations, advanced analytics teams and business leaders are often considered to be residents of different universes. There is frequently a disconnect between the practical needs, priorities, and expectations of team business and team analytics, preventing the parties from developing a partnership or gaining a mutual understanding of one another.[42]

A lack of effective collaboration between management and the advanced analytics team is typically the result of conventional, hierarchical business structures. Too often, the upper echelons of leadership set goals for process furtherance initiatives, innovation, and product enhancements without inviting others to participate in the decision-making process. In advanced analytics projects, management's failure to maintain close collaboration with the analytics practitioners on the ground may reflect a lack of understanding of how the analytics team operates and the insights it can bring.

If you were really into sci-fiction, you might remark that team business is living in the Milky Way and team analytics is in the middle of Andromeda. These silos seem to exist as alternate realities (or separate galaxies) to which only a few esteemed interlopers may have reciprocal access.

In the boardroom, senior executives often cannot articulate the benefits of analytics when decisions are being made, since very few have direct experience. They may spend hours participating in "design thinking" workshops or experimenting with project prioritization matrices, fishbone charts, and flavor-of-the-day business management models, but without analytics insight they will fail to grasp what is possible. Instead, they will continue to perpetuate and repurpose existing frameworks, processes, and technology, their horizons limited to what they already know.

Senior executives may also fail to foresee the complexities involved in adopting newer technology. They tend not to recognize that embedding advanced analytics models in existing processes and systems to improve efficiency and accuracy will require upgrades to legacy data management systems. Even if they do accept that upgrades are needed, they may be resistant to making the necessary upfront investment in enterprise technologies to eliminate system constraints and bottlenecks and propel innovation. Thus, analytics efforts may be hampered from the start by a failure of imagination and a lack of support and resources.

The problem continues once business goals have been set, when the gap between team business and team analytics can impede their execution. Without open lines of communication between the two sides, business goals may be filtered through successive layers of management before they reach an organization's engineers. By the time the requirements and objectives set for the analytics team actually reach team analytics, their original impetus or focus may be lost. The problem becomes more convoluted in organizations where a single metric or KPI may mean different things to different people. Vernacular barriers may also arise between business leaders and the engineers working on advanced analytics projects.

---

42   https://hbr.org/2020/02/are-your-companys-leaders-and-data-scientists-on-the-same-page

Advanced analytics practitioners often feel thwarted by organizational barriers that mean they are not privy to the state of the business, the budget cycle, and the tools and practices used throughout the organization. When analytics professionals are blocked from gaining a clear view of the organizational picture and the problems their analytics model is intended to solve in dollars and cents, critical opportunities are missed.

The analytics team may be ready and able to grapple with advanced analytics model accuracy, optimization, robustness, model scalability, and myriad other issues but, without a window into the full organizational picture, its mission will be hindered by knowledge gaps. Such gaps hamper operational excellence, impede the embedding of analytics in business processes, and make success elusive. They also breed misunderstanding and mistrust, causing the chasm to widen as each team becomes increasingly frustrated with the other's modus operandi and unable to find common ground.

Fortunately, the technology to build bridges between team analytics and team business has already been developed. No! No! Not by a data-savvy tech giant, but by Homo sapiens in Africa between 50,000 and 150,000 years ago, when they developed human language to communicate.

Organizations must find creative ways to use this capability to bridge the gap between business and analytics teams. The advanced analytics team's mission is to uncover insights that will solve business problems, so it requires the help of those on the business side of the organization to identify which insights will be contextually valuable and actionable.

The analytics team must be armed with management's crystal-clear assessment of the current state of the company's systems and processes; a systematic, suitable analytical approach; and short-term and long-term goals and strategies. In addition to contributing these insights, senior executives must be involved in D&A strategy because the practical reality is that it is generally management that controls budgeting and resources and is in charge of business transformations, while analytics practitioners and technology experts usually are not.

Because analytics problem framing requires advanced analytics skills, however, team analytics is far from a subordinate partner in this enterprise. The business team must rely on the insight of senior analytics architects and others who have technical expertise and can navigate the analytics architecture and data issues.

Roadmaps should be developed that include milestones and concrete plans for each step that will be taken on the path to analytics transformation. Periodic assessments should be conducted, focusing on whether short-term and long-term goals have been met and milestones reached. Teams should have the flexibility to rework the overall strategy when a change in direction is warranted. As needed, strategic plans should be regularly recalibrated to factor in the organization's culture and risk tolerance, its management of employee culture shock, and the extent to which it has been effective in executing technology improvements. Each of these requirements demands open communication between team business and team analytics at every turn.

But who are the ambassadors from these disparate realms who will build this much-needed bridge between them?

Bridge-Builders: Installing the Right People

Executive Sponsor

Extensive research still has not been performed to discern the key leadership traits required for the successful implementation of AI in business. We do know, however, that a leadership cadre or executive sponsor should be assigned to the digital analytics transformation effort, with responsibility for providing a proper budget, resources, external consulting, and training for the project.[43] The executive sponsor will provide important parameters for the project, such as available funding, and will advise on organizational culture and other pertinent issues.

CAOs, CDOs, Data Stewards and Data Owners

Organizations committed to digital analytics transformation clearly need highly skilled technical talent to tackle all facets of data collection, management, and analysis. In many cases, companies are also adding positions that embody a merging of business and analytics insight, such as chief analytics officer (CAO) and chief data officer (CDO), as well as data stewards and data owners.

The creation of a chief analytics officer (CAO) position is one important step in facilitating collaboration between team analytics and team business. In bridging the gap between the two teams, the CAO is ideally positioned to help cement a common vision and a shared set of objectives for an analytics project. The CAO role is especially important in organizations where AI is not the core business but instead plays a supporting role, helping to drive operational excellence and operations innovation. Linking the right analytics, data, and software technologies to the appropriate business needs and outcomes can be an arduous task. The CAO should therefore be instrumental in facilitating frequent communication between the data scientists and engineers and the business team. The CAO can also provide advice on which product features can be delivered given current platform capabilities.

CAOs can function as evangelists, sharing their knowledge and articulating the nuances of AI technology and helping knowledge workers to understand and appreciate the value generated by advanced analytics. In the absence of communication or guiding principles from the upper echelon of leadership, the CAO can highlight the reasons why automation or advanced analytics is critical and what success looks like. The CAO can also share the exact reasons behind the organization's decision to switch course from age-old manual business processes to automation. By helping to build bridges between team business and team analytics, the CAO can bring the organization closer to the Data as a Horizontal paradigm.

---

43   https://hbr.org/sponsored/2021/04/the-state-of-digital-adoption-2021

The Data Governance Team

In the last decade, there has been a heavy focus on data governance and data literacy, and a move to adopt a single source of truth (SSOT) paradigm. As part of the effort to establish an SSOT, organizations handling troves of data typically lay out a set of doctrines called data governance policies.

"Data governance ensures secure availability of high-quality data to enable integrated data management and principled governance." [44]

Key data leaders in an organization typically collaborate to form a data governance committee that drafts comprehensive policy guidelines to manage the data life cycle and support external compliance. Data regulations such as GDPR (the EU's Global Data Protection Regulation), CCPA (the California Consumer Privacy Act), and HIPAA (the Health Insurance Portability and Accountability Act of 1996) must be factored in when data collection is initiated, and the data governance committee should lead that function, while also supporting the organization's data strategy and vision.

The contents of data governance policies will be unique to each individual organization and the mission of its data governance committee, but certain vital objectives should be covered in these doctrines (*Fig. 32*):

- Protect and secure a variety of data categories
- Draft comprehensive privacy and compliance policy guidelines
- Ensure data life cycle management is consistent and efficient
- Manage risk associated with data assets
- Support Data and Analytics (D&A) strategy and vision
- Facilitate high-quality data accessibility
- Organize an integrated data architecture

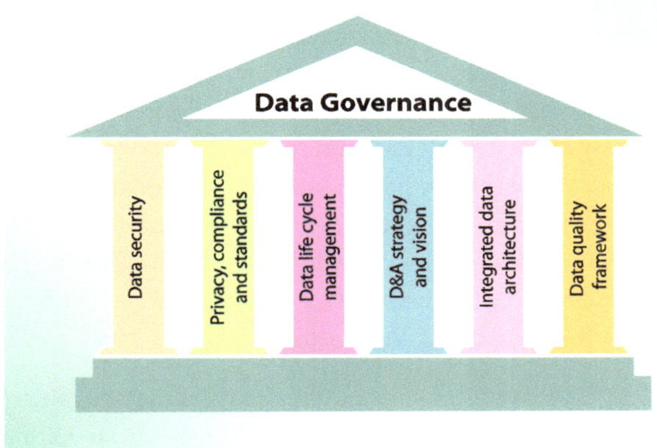

Fig. 32: Data governance covenants

---

44   https://cio.ubc.ca/data-governance/data-governance-program

Data custodians, data stewards, data owners and chief data officers (CDOs) play pivotal roles in an organization's data governance team. As a business grows, it is the responsibility of the data custodian (who manages the technical environment in which the data resides) to ensure that its data is secure, without breaches in privacy and security. Since security breaches lead to revenue loss and significant erosion in customers' brand confidence, organizations have invested heavily in AI engines to ramp up the quality of the cybersecurity products they build.

While it is the role of the chief data officer (CDO) to make sure that data governance strategies are in place, data owners are responsible for maintaining the data within their purview and ensuring it is fit for its purpose. A data steward, unlike the CDO, typically holds the hands-on data governance responsibilities in an organization. The data steward is responsible for the quality of the outputs for the collective sum of organizational data pipelines, data sources, and tables. These include terminology alignment, standardization, security, regulatory compliance, and the accessibility of all corporate data. An organization will typically have one CDO, one data steward, and multiple data owners. For an organization to succeed in AI initiatives, a superb data governance policy and rigorous execution are a must.

According to the Big Data and AI Executive Survey 2021, 65% of mainstream organizations have adopted a CDO role.[45] This statistic represents a 45% percent jump from a decade ago. The report notes, however, that the majority of CDOs are still grappling with their roles, responsibilities, single point accountability, CDO organizational reporting structures, and areas of focus.

The Analytics Team

Now we come to the pivotal roles that deliver the actual advanced analytics expertise to an organization. To gain a thorough understanding of these, we must look first at the academic disciplines from which they emerged.

Data science is used as a catchall term to refer to advances in data analytics and innovation related to AI, ML, and IoT. However, so many different meanings and implications have been attributed to the term that it has been distorted over time. There are heated debates in academic and industry research circles around the vocabulary of data science and how various terms are conflated in business communication and in definitions that suit the purposes of other disciplines. Marketing strategies employed by consulting companies and analytics products companies, and loose terminology spouted by AI spin doctors and self-professed AI aficionados on social media, have created yet more confusion about what these terms mean, further limiting how effective they can be.

Alan Garber, in a 2019 MIT Press article, eloquently articulates the struggle around defining data science: *"The pervasive use of the term 'data science' in academic settings reflects both*

---

45   Randy Bean and Thomas Davenport, "Big Data and AI Executive Survey, Executive Summary of Findings," January 2021

the appeal of the intellectual activities it encompasses and the capaciousness—or vagueness—of its meaning. The collection, organization, analysis, and interpretation of data can all be considered its domain."[46]

Thomas Davenport's commentary on Alan Garner's article further highlights the challenges associated with untangling what data science (DS) is or what data scientists do in a business setting: *"It is probably safe to say that academics care more about clear definitions of disciplines and terms than do business people. There may be even less clarity about what constitutes data science and data scientists in the business domain."*[47]

Instead of considering DS as a discipline, it is best to consider it as an umbrella term that refers to an amalgamation of ML, statistics, computer science, data engineering, data architecture, software engineering, software architecture, organizational strategy, and business activities (*Fig. 33*). DS can be described as a complex multi-step analytical process or an analytics life cycle that starts with a business problem to solve using *data*. Data engineering, data systems, databases, analysis, experimentation, verification, validation, and data literacy-related activities are as important as computation methods and generalized pattern matching.

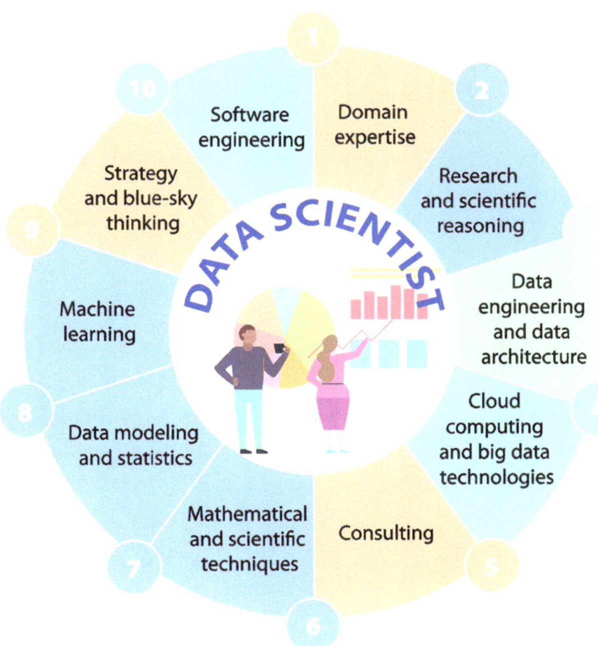

Fig. 33: Data scientist competencies

46   https://hdsr.mitpress.mit.edu/pub/pjl0jtkp/release/6

47   https://www.tomdavenport.com/beyond-unicorns-educating-classifying-and-certifying-business-data-scientists/

According to an article published by *Harvard Business Review* in 2021, as little as one-quarter of one percent of the world knows how to code.[48] Data scientists with competencies at the intersection of software and data engineering, and with experience in state-of-the-art, free, open-source statistics, software, database, and cloud technology are in short supply and hence command premium dollars in the competitive marketplace.

U.S. Bureau of Labor Statistics researchers project strong growth (31–35%) in the field of data science through 2030.[49] In 2022, Glassdoor ranked data scientist as the third most desired job in the United States, citing more than 6,500 job openings.[50] Organizations are racing to hire data scientists despite the business world's limited comprehension of what DS is or what a data scientist should do when hired. Often, prospective employers are taken in by the MBA-ification and fetishization of AI, ML, and DS in everything from media and marketing blogs to respected business journals. *Harvard Business Review* helped fuel the hype in 2012 with a bold headline: "Data Scientist: The Sexiest Job of the 21st Century." [51]

In a follow-up 2022 *Harvard Business Review* article by the same authors of the 2012 piece, titled "Is Data Scientist Still the Sexiest Job of the 21st Century?", the authors affirm their earlier statement, asserting that the role is more in demand than ever.[52] They attribute this continuing trend to the increasing popularity of AI in business and the certainty expressed by companies of all sizes, and in all locations, that they need data scientists to develop AI models. Will data science still be the sexiest job in 2032? An educated guess suggests that the same role will still be held at a premium but that its name may be upgraded to an even more gimmicky title that further fires up the popular imagination, perhaps one that alludes to sophisticated software embedded with AI.

Hiring Advanced Analytics Engineers

In their attempts to attract analytics talent, human resources business units have repurposed existing organizational titles, such as program manager, project manager, business analyst, data analyst, product manager, business intelligence (BI) manager, and other reporting DS roles. One regularly sees job postings calling for candidates who have decades of experience and expertise in a particular technology that has been around for less than a couple of years. Other postings demand simultaneous expertise in ten ML algorithms, software engineering, data engineering, and data architecture, a wish list that is not feasible.

Most organizations are unable to appreciate what AI, DS, and ML actually mean, and the capabilities they offer. They also lack the know-how to hire and retain quality talent, and don't invest enough in technology and technology awareness.

---

48   https://hbr.org/2021/11/how-no-code-platforms-can-bring-ai-to-small-and-midsize-businesses
49   https://www.bls.gov/emp/tables/fastest-growing-occupations.htm
50   https://www.glassdoor.com/List/Best-Jobs-in-America-LST_KQ0,20.htm
51   https://hbr.org/2012/10/data-scientist-the-sexiest-job-of-the-21st-century
52   https://hbr.org/2022/07/is-data-scientist-still-the-sexiest-job-of-the-21st-century

Universities have been churning out DS and ML masters and doctoral graduates to meet industry demand.[53] Unfortunately, academia would better prepare students to be successful in the workforce if schools would offer upgraded curricula focused on the practical application of their skills. Why is this so? Newly minted data scientists with doctoral or master's degrees are not "road-ready." They often need on-the-ground training or real-world practice to contextualize and translate the pure academic research or AI theory they have learned into business outcomes. Introducing a one-year practicum in the industry as a requisite for graduation would greatly improve the prospects of emerging data scientists. For-profit educational institutions have been touting expensive snake oil in the form of six- to twelve-week "expert" DS boot camps that capitalize on the demand for seasoned data practitioners. These programs are falling short, however, and road-ready data scientists remain a scarce commodity.

The market has seen an influx of (less cost-prohibitive) candidates masquerading as experienced data scientists: recent graduates applying with a fly-by-night DS bootcamp education or managers who only have experience with no-code, drag-and-drop AI proprietary technologies. To weed out these applicants, savvy engineering-focused organizations are posting job openings for advanced analytics engineer roles. The ideal advanced analytics engineer, also referred to as an analytics engineer, is a skilled polymath with expertise in computer science, data engineering, statistics, and ML, who also has strong business acumen. Most recruiters explicitly look for Ph.D.'s for advanced analytics roles, due to their anticipated creativity, problem-solving skills, independence, and project ownership capabilities.

Retaining Advanced Analytics Engineers

When organizations manage to find and hire their coveted data scientists (or advanced analytics engineers), they often find it a challenge to retain them. Organizational leaders learning about AI's potential for business transformation may push the advanced analytics team too hard and may expect too much too soon from the data scientists they have hired. Often, these data scientists are expected to perform miracles despite being given poorly framed business questions, bad data, and insufficient raw materials (data and infrastructure) for modeling. These factors, and the ambiguous career paths often laid out for data scientists, are often cited as reasons for attrition.[54]

The following statistics shed some light on the challenges of hiring and retaining qualified data scientists. According to a report published by QuantHub in 2020[55]:

- As of 2020, the shortage of data scientists in the United States was estimated at 250,000
- The average data scientist turnover is approximately two years

53   https://fortune.com/education/information-technology/masters/rankings/best-masters-in-data-science/

54   https://omdena.com/blog/why-data-scientists-leave-their-jobs/

55   https://quanthub.com/data-scientist-shortage-2020/

- Job postings outnumber job searches by a multiple of three
- With each new position, data scientists receive an average salary increase of 14%
- The global tech talent shortage is set to increase to 85 million by 2030
- Annual AI-related hiring growth between 2015 and 2019 was 74%
- In 2020, 83% of companies were investing in Big Data projects

Further exacerbating the shortage of data scientists is the phenomenon referred to as the Great Resignation of 2021, an aftermath of the Covid-19 pandemic.[56,57] According to an article from the U.S. Bureau of Labor Statistics, in November 2021 alone, more than 6.3 million Americans voluntarily quit their jobs (up 382,000 from the previous month), the highest level ever recorded since these data were first produced in December 2000.[58]

Advanced Analytics Engineering Titles, Roles and Responsibilities

Organizations that struggle to exploit the full potential of their data assets often surround their advanced analytics practitioners with non-specialist managers who lack technical knowledge.[59] Sequestering advanced analytics practitioners within organizational silos and failing to leverage data assets are common mistakes. It is advisable for organizations to avoid pigeonholing their data scientists if they wish to fuse domain expertise, business acumen, and technical know-how. This fusion of capabilities can only be accomplished by connecting data scientists more directly with upper-echelon business leaders who can convey a nuanced understanding of the business problems they need to solve.[60]

Instead of expecting a single engineer who happens to possess the necessary expertise and skill sets in the relevant disciplines to serve as the sole bridge between the analytics team and the business-focused teams, businesses should form an integrated team of analytics professionals with non-overlapping, complementary skill sets, all directed toward the same business goals.

An MIT press article published by Kolaczyk et.al. gives some examples of key DS roles that organizations must invest in if they want to realize their DS/AI ambitions:

1. The DS developer (or modeler), who would be the core developer with a stronger focus on DS methodologies and techniques.
2. The DS engineer, who would focus on data piping, data quality, and data ingestion for the purpose of DS modeling.
3. The DS architect, who would have a deeper understanding of platforms and data enterprise architecture for end-to-end operationalization.

56   https://www.pwc.com/gx/en/issues/workforce/hopes-and-fears-2022.html
57   https://www.pewresearch.org/fact-tank/2022/03/09/majority-of-workers-who-quit-a-job-in-2021-cite-low-pay-no-opportunities-for-advancement-feeling-disrespected/
58   https://www.bls.gov/opub/ted/2022/number-of-quits-at-all-time-high-in-november-2021.htm
59   https://www.ft.com/content/49e81ebe-cbc3-11e7-8536-d321d0d897a3
60   https://hbr.org/2018/12/what-great-data-analysts-do-and-why-every-organization-needs-them

4. The DS storyteller, who would have a stronger focus on data visualization and DS communication and possess strong business process acumen.[61]

It is worth emphasizing that titles and roles will vary depending on an organization's size and its maturity level in the Analytics Fitness framework, as well as its sector, technology and available resources, and the analytics savvy of its executive leadership, to name just a few factors.

New titles continue to emerge along with the push for embedded analytics and end-to-end process AI. One of the most recent of these roles—advanced analytics architect—requires "full-stack" data scientists (those with a mastery of analytics, statistics, machine learning, and software data engineering, as well as business acumen).[62] These analytics professionals bring formal and rigorous software engineering best practices to the data science function, while providing avenues for the simultaneous amalgamation of value-driven business outcomes with an analytical mindset.[56]

Attracting candidates with advanced analytics skills, including experience in cloud computing and Big Data technologies, is vitally important for an organization's digital analytics transformation initiatives. Integrating and embedding analytics talent in organizational verticals such as engineering, finance, sales, and marketing will bring numerous advantages. The presence of employees with these skill sets at all organizational levels will enable businesses to design and manufacture superior products; explore untapped markets; improve product branding, upselling, and cross-selling; and ultimately generate more revenue.

Maximizing the Value of Advanced Analytics Engineers

When one looks closely at what advanced analytics engineers (commonly referred to as data scientists) in competent, data-driven organizations currently do, one finds that most of their time is spent doing foundational data work to set in place the precursors needed for robust analytics.[63] An 80/20 formula is often used to describe the workload of an advanced analytics engineer. More than 80% of their time is spent on tasks that lay the foundation for the implementation and adoption of analytics models. Advanced analytics engineers are expected to find organizational or external data; clean, validate, and verify data; and build data pipelines. They are also tasked with ensuring organizational alignment on data terminology; playing a consultative role to bridge organizational technology gaps; working with data engineers and data architects to productionize manual data-related processes; and educating business colleagues on new technology, automation, and the adoption of new processes.

The need for such comprehensive groundwork means that only 5 to 20% of an engineer's time is left for building ML models and making personalized data products for customers.

61   https://hdsr.mitpress.mit.edu/pub/gblp1ru7/release/1#nfbye7bkr02

62   https://locallyoptimistic.com/post/analytics-engineer/

63   https://www.techrepublic.com/article/data-science-skills-gap/

As mentioned earlier, according to a 2015 publication by Google researchers Sculley et al., this number is generally closer to 5%.[64]

Fortunately, this problem can be alleviated by organizational investment in building a robust unified analytics platform (UAP). As we have discussed previously, a UAP furnishes an ecosystem for the seamless collection, storage, and analysis of data, assembling it into a format that can be furnished as inputs to advanced analytics models. A UAP obviates much of the laborious groundwork described above, freeing up the bandwidth of advanced analytics practitioners. The skills of these expert engineers can then be channeled more fruitfully into complex modeling and other sophisticated tasks that can move the organization forward in its Analytics Fitness journey.

The adoption of commercial data solutions from vendors such as Data Bricks, Starburst, StarDog, Snowflake, Talend, Teradata, Microsoft Azure, and Amazon Web Services can also be valuable in facilitating this effort. These technologies provide better tools to improve data quality, thereby freeing advanced analytics practitioners to focus more of their time on building superior models required to optimize business processes and improve efficiency.

As organizations reach the higher levels of the Advanced Analytics Fitness framework, they will be better able to design roles that harness the skills and meet the career aspirations of the new class of advanced analytics and AI practitioners. These organizations will be well positioned to create appropriate advanced analytics roles and titles and establish career paths that place the most experienced and business savvy practitioners in upper management roles. In addition to providing a more rewarding career path for highly qualified analytics professionals, the elevation of these experts into the upper echelons of leadership will remedy the shortage of technical skills and insight typically found in the C-suite.[65]

Data Literacy

Breaking down silos, fostering communication between team analytics and team business, and filling organizational roles such as CAO and CDO to support this linkage are vital steps for organizations looking to revolutionize their business through analytics. Ensuring that "unicorn" analytics engineers are supported by an integrated team of data professionals is another important piece of the puzzle. But there is an additional, critical step businesses can take to ignite the spread of a thriving data culture: fostering data literacy. Data literacy has the important benefit of freeing advanced analytics professionals from having to play a de facto role as educators in analytics skills and concepts throughout their organizations. Even more critically, facilitating the spread of data literacy skills advances the democratization of data and can move a business closer to the *Data as a Horizontal* paradigm.

---

64   https://papers.nips.cc/paper/2015/file/86df7dcfd896fcaf2674f757a2463eba-Paper.pdf
65   https://www.ft.com/content/49e81ebe-cbc3-11e7-8536-d321d0d897a3

Data literacy is becoming a popular term in industry and academic circles. Data literacy is simply the ability to "speak" data—to work with it, interpret it and analyze it. According to a 2019 report by Gartner, 80% of all organizations will include data literacy in their D&A strategy and change management programs by 2023.[66]

Data literacy allows individuals to:

- Make data-driven and fact-based decisions
- Access data and perform data discovery
- Collect, manipulate, organize, and manage data
- Identify and manage data flaws
- Be adept in exploratory data analysis (EDA)
- Be competent in visual and verbal storytelling
- Delineate relevant and irrelevant information
- Yield insights and action-oriented analysis
- Verify and validate information presented
- Identify logic flaws in statistical information presented
- Question data and information provenance
- Frame the right business questions
- Be empowered and effective in their job functions, regardless of their prior level of technical education and savvy
- Absorb the shocks associated with organizational technology shifts
- Implement descriptive analytics and monitor, measure, and iterate
- Support data privacy, data security, and data ethics

Data literacy is such a vital skill in today's information landscape that middle schools and high schools are identifying ways to incorporate it into their curricula.[67] In businesses, spreading data literacy is key to building a healthy data culture and effectively leveraging advanced analytics. Data literacy provides employees with a functional grasp of analytics concepts and capabilities that can help free them from the performance of automatable and repetitive tasks and enable them to pivot to new areas where they can leverage analytical and strategic mindsets.[68]

Allocating the necessary time and budget for employee upskilling is key to building a culture of transparency and knowledge dissemination. Providing employees with adequate analytics training promotes their deeper engagement with the business, its markets and its customers, and their investment in and alignment with the organization's strategic goals. This investment will, in turn, nudge the organization toward becoming more collaborative and primed for analytics projects. Providing information forums to share data discovery within functional groups will create opportunities for employees in those groups to help

---

66   https://blogs.gartner.com/andrew_white/2019/01/03/our-top-data-and-analytics-predicts-for-2019/

67   https://hbr.org/2020/02/boost-your-teams-data-literacy

68   https://www.ey.com/en_gl/consulting/tech-horizon-survey

refine analytics goals and end-products. Data, logic, and evidence-based reasoning will then become an ever-evolving blueprint that spans every part of the organization.

In addition to promoting data literacy internally, hiring data-literate employees from outside is an important way to further the dissemination of this vital skill. According to a 2022 research report from Qlik, a data and analytics integration platform company, data literacy will be the most in-demand skill by 2030 as AI transforms global workplaces.[69] The report, "Data Literacy: The Upskilling Evolution," notes that 85% of executives believe data literacy will become as vital in the future as the ability to use a computer is today.

Because higher levels of data literacy help to reduce culture shock around the adoption of analytics products, data literacy is a concept often associated with the final stages of the analytics operationalization and change management process. Indeed, data literacy performs a critical function in analytics product operationalization and adoption. The data literacy of an organization's broad employee population can prime them to accept and utilize analytics technology. Just as importantly, a firm grasp of data concepts by business leaders can aid them in executing effective change management initiatives that do more than simply attempt to retrofit analytics products into existing processes. But data literacy is a factor that should be addressed long before the rollout of a new analytics product and the launch of accompanying change management efforts.

Contributor to this book Stephen Gatchell makes the critical point that deferring data literacy efforts across an organization until the later stages of analytics implementation is a mistake. In an article that can be found in the Appendix of this book, Gatchell makes the argument that data literacy sets the stage for the development of a successful data strategy and for every step that follows, and that it should be included as a budget line item and as a key priority at the outset of any analytics project. Some of these concepts are also revisited in Chapter 8 (*Prototype to Analytics Product*).

To Summarize:

In this chapter, we discussed the human face of analytics transformation. We looked at the role of analytics practitioners in the business environment and the vital importance of close collaboration between team analytics and team business in setting D&A strategy. We also examined the full range of human resources needed to support robust analytics, from data governance personnel to the hard-to-find "full-stack" advanced analytics engineer.

Essential Takeaways:

- Data literacy means being able to work with, interpret and analyze data.
- Data democratization is the concept of providing and disseminating non-sensitive organizational data to all employees and equipping them with data to be highly effective in their job functions.

---

69   https://www.qlik.com/us/-/media/files/resource-library/global-us/direct/datasheets/ds-data-literacy-the-upskilling-evolution-en.pdf

- Most organizations are unable to appreciate what AI, DS, and ML actually mean, and the capabilities they offer. They also lack the know-how to hire and retain quality talent, and don't invest enough in technology and technology awareness.
- Between 80 and 95 percent of a data scientist's time is typically spent on tasks that finding organizational or external data; cleaning, validating, and verifying data; building data pipelines; getting alignment on data terminology; playing a consultative role to bridge organizational technology gaps; working with data engineers and data architects to productionize manual data-related processes, and educating business colleagues on new technology, automation and the adoption of new processes.
- As organizations move up higher in the Analytics Fitness framework, they will be better able to design roles that harness the skills and meet the career aspirations of the new class of advanced analytics and AI practitioners.
- Organizations handling troves of data outline a set of doctrines called data governance policies. Key data leaders in the organization collaborate to form a data governance committee, which drafts comprehensive policy guidelines to manage the data life cycle and support external compliance.
  - The chief data officer (CDO) makes sure organizational data governance strategies are in place.
  - Data owners are responsible for defining data and ensuring it is fit for its intended purpose.
  - The data steward is responsible for the quality of data sources and tables, including terminology alignment, standardization, security, regulatory compliance, and the accessibility of organizational data.

Chapter 6

Managing Data for Transformational Analytics

In the cloud culture, we have transitioned from megabytes on hard disks to terabytes on disk arrays to petabytes as data management technologies evolve to keep pace with the multitude of unstructured data streams generated at the intersection of our physical and digital worlds through the Internet of Things (IoT) (*Fig. 34*).

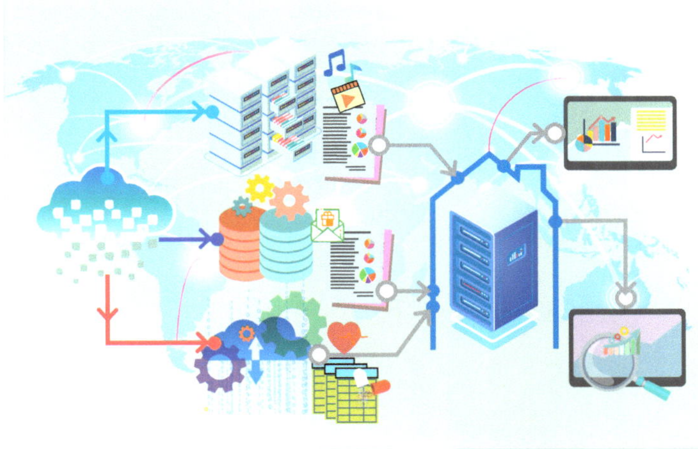

Fig. 34: Representation of a digitally connected world generating various data streams

As these data management technologies advance, the costs of data storage and computing power decline and their accessibility increases. More and more businesses are taking advantage of data-driven insights as they seek to boost efficiency and stabilize their profitability by minimizing costs, reducing customer attrition, and accelerating business processes. The proliferation of new data management systems can itself be a challenge, however, as organizations struggle to stay up to date and grapple with decisions about which of the rapidly growing range of data storage and management solutions will best meet their needs.

In this chapter, we will examine the evolution of data storage, management, and processing technologies. We will see how these technologies have evolved from relational databases and first-generation enterprise data warehouses to the newer, decentralized solutions that data-savvy companies are currently adopting to manage and process their data. The pages that follow will introduce some terms that may be unfamiliar. The goal of this chapter is not to make you an expert in relational databases or cloud computing but, instead, to equip you with the vocabulary the engineers you work with will typically use.

Data Storage and Management

Data Warehouses

First-generation data platforms, also known as enterprise data warehouses (EDWs or DWs) are relational databases, or collections of relational databases. In these databases, an organization's past and current business data is integrated from multiple streams, processed, summarized, and stored (*Fig. 35*). DWs, which became popular in the 1980s, consist of data tables or schemas that contain an organization's relevant business metrics—in structured form—which can be used in descriptive analytics for organizational metrics reporting. Engineers and managers can retrieve (read) information from data tables by performing a step known as querying. A programming language called structured query language (SQL) was developed by IBM in the 1970s to manage and find relationships between structured data. Oracle, PostgreSQL, and MySQL are commonly used structured (preformatted) databases found in traditional data warehouses.

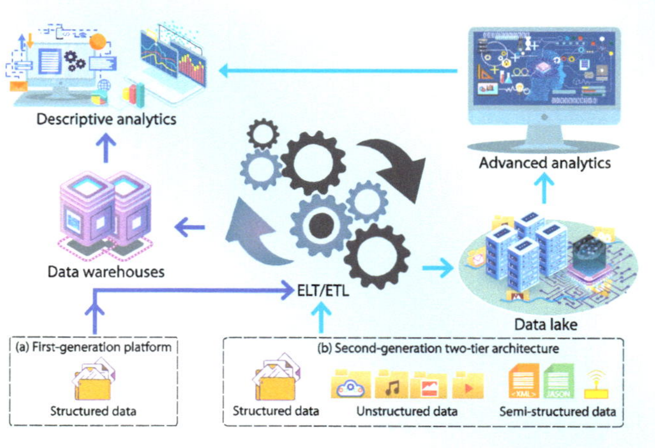

Fig. 35. First- (DW) and second-generation (data lake) storage platforms

As we discussed in Chapter 4 (*The Analytics Triad™: Goals, Metrics, and Data & Analytics Strategy*), first-generation DWs composed of relational databases present certain strategic limitations, in that they can only handle structured data, thereby restricting users to descriptive analytics or BI applications. In addition, first-generation DWs are hampered by a limited storage capacity that makes them poorly suited to handling torrents of data. Second-generation, cloud-based data warehouses remove the limitations of physical data centers and can scale to handle large volumes of data. They also obviate many of the performance issues that hinder traditional DWs.

In modern DWs, software as a service (SaaS) solutions such as Snowflake can provide flexibility in storing machine-generated data from various ever-expanding sources, such as mobile and sensors. Their popularity has grown in the last few years, as they provide support for flexible schemas. They are suitable for building analytic solutions that are faster and easier to use than traditional DW offerings.[70,71] They support the storage of semi-structured data formats such as JSON, Avro, ORC, Parquet, and XML without transformation.[72] Semi-structured data is a form of structured data that does not conform to a tabular structure but still contains tags or other markers that identify individual, distinct entities within the data (*Fig. 36*).

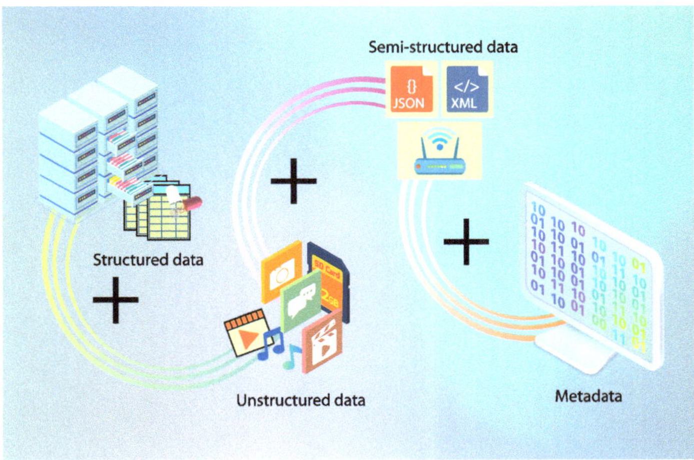

Fig. 36: Data taxonomy – structured, unstructured, and semi-structured data

Organizations use DWs as information platforms. Data warehousing offers precise, consistent, validated data across systems and business spheres. For example, an analytics professional working on a project related to customer experience can use a DW as a one-stop data shop for gaining an integrated view of troves of data from disparate data silos within a business. An organization may store billing information, customer product purchase information, customer contract information, customer engagement data, marketing campaign data, and customer loyalty points, for example.

---

70   https://docs.snowflake.com/en/user-guide/intro-key-concepts.html

71   https://www.infoworld.com/article/3663700/snowflake-switches-gears-from-data-warehouse-to-application-cloud.html

72   https://docs.snowflake.com/en/user-guide/semistructuredconcepts

In addition to providing crucial business metrics for the performance of day-to-day operations, DWs also capture metadata. Metadata (data about data) contains information and characteristics of the data, so data users understand the source of the data, how it made its way to the tables in the DW, and what assumptions and business rules were applied to summarize the data. Metadata provenance and management are vital in siloed organizations, where there can be multiple copies of the same data repurposed for various business use cases across multiple infrastructure silos.

Extract, Transform, Load (ETL)

ETL is the process by which data is extracted (*Extract*) from various source systems, converted (*Transform*) into a predetermined format, and stored (*Load*) in DWs *(Fig. 37)*. ETL loads torrents of data from both internal and external systems into an organizational DW. The format of the data stored in the DW in this way is highly optimized to be used for analytics workloads.

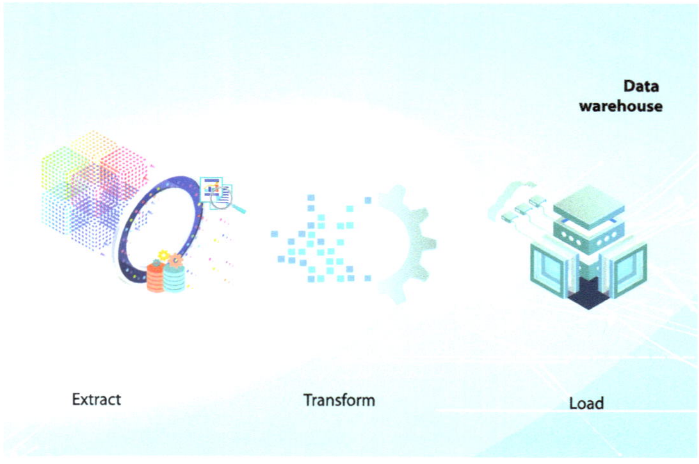

Fig. 37: Extract, transform, load (ETL) process

Data Lakes

Data lakes are second-generation data repositories that can store an organization's structured data and a wide range of unprocessed, raw, unstructured data. The following figure highlights the critical differences between DWs and data lakes *(Fig. 38)*.

Fig. 38: Data warehouse (DW) vs. data lake

Second-generation Big Data unified analytics platforms with data lakes can support advanced analytics research and development (R&D) efforts. Organizations using these modalities can innovate rapidly and gain a competitive advantage in the marketplace.

Extract, Load, Transform (ELT)

With the recent technological advances in cloud-based data storage solutions, an *extract, load, transform* (ELT) paradigm is emerging. This development has been fueled by the elastic nature of cloud-based DWs, which reduce the resource constraints for storing and converting raw data into required formats. ELT reverses the last two steps in the ETL process. After extracting the data (Extract), ELT loads (*Load*) and then transforms (*Transform*) the data (*Fig. 39*). By swapping the last two operations and pushing the transformation step to the target database for better performance, ELT offers flexibility, speed, and ease of storage, making it beneficial for Big Data and AI applications. Snowflake and Talend offer the flexibility to handle both ETL and ELT workloads.

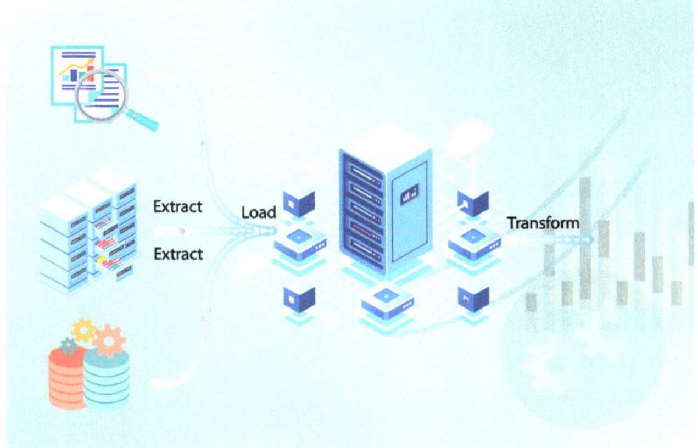

Fig. 39: Representation of extract, load, transform (ELT) process

Next-Generation Data Management

In recent years, skepticism has emerged concerning centralized forms of data architecture, largely driven by tech-savvy, data-mature organizations that focus on advanced analytics and posit that the single source of truth (SSOT) paradigm may inhibit flexibility and access to data and may not be sufficiently customizable for advanced analytics projects.

The SSOT is designed to maintain high data quality, governance, and data literacy. However, critics warn that a top-down, master data management approach could stifle innovation, research and development (R&D) efforts, and strategic organizational growth, potentially reversing progress made toward data democratization. According to proponents of this view, processes established to support the SSOT paradigm may be unsuited to a broader D&A strategy or complex advanced analytics workloads and may need to be redesigned and recalibrated.

EDWs and data lakes, which are, respectively, first- and second-generation storage platforms, have come in for the same criticism, as they fall into the category of traditional, centralized, monolithic data infrastructure, where one business vertical, typically IT (information technology), manages all the organizational data.[73] These platforms are tied to specific data technologies and maintained and driven by hyper-specialized (and centralized) engineers. The engineers in the business vertical control all data ingestion and pipeline and transformation efforts.

In 2019, an architectural design pattern called a data lakehouse was developed in the research labs of Stanford University, UC Berkeley and Databricks to combine the best characteristics of data warehouses and data lakes. Open source and commercial versions of data lakehouse architecture, often referred to as a third-generation storage platform, are available.[74] Data lakehouses provide open, direct access to data formats such as Apache Parquet and ORC, yield improved performance and reliability, and support compute- and memory-intensive advanced analytics workloads for which neither data lakes nor DWs are ideal. In the data lakehouse architecture paradigm, once you load the data into a data lakehouse, there is no need to load the data into a DW for analytics workloads. Instead, the user can directly query the data, which resides in a form of cheaper but highly reliable storage known as object stores, thus reducing the operational overhead on data pipelines.

Another new generation of data management and storage solutions is now emerging, as part of this paradigm shift in the way organizations handle their data.[75] *Data mesh* and *ubiquitous data* are new conceptual models that go beyond the older, centralized D&A infrastructure model and team rubrics.

---

73   https://www.softlanding.ca/blog/data-mesh-a-fresh-approach-to-data-organization/
74   https://www.cidrdb.org/cidr2021/papers/cidr2021_paper17.pdf
75   https://martinfowler.com/articles/data-monolith-to-mesh.html

Data Mesh

A *data mesh*, a distributed data architecture concept introduced by Zhamak Dehghani, is a type of data platform that organizes enterprise data architecture around separate business domains. Its architecture accommodates the building of domain-specific data pipelines. The data domains are responsible for curation of their own data, which is made accessible via API and shared across analytics teams. Each business unit only links and collates data from the DWs of other coordinated business units when needed. This model is particularly helpful for scalability and rapid adaptation to technological advancements in the D&A space.

A data mesh platform can better handle the *ubiquity of data* in today's enterprises—the massive data sets collected and generated across every part of an organization.

The concept of data mesh is premised upon the idea that, as the amount and complexity of data an organization collects increases, it is prudent to partially shift domain data ownership and responsibility for the selection of D&A technology to each individual domain. "Why?" you may ask. The data engineers, architects, analytics practitioners, and subject matter experts (SMEs) tied to a business domain have in-depth knowledge of that domain's business processes, data pipelines, data ingestion, data wrangling, transformation workflow, and business logic. They possess the experience and the domain-specific expertise to be agile and to evolve, innovate and adapt rapidly to technological market shifts, thereby boosting the overall agility of the organization.

Data mesh allows for highly coordinated cross-domain collaboration and distributed ownership of organizational data. It reduces the excessive centralization, scalability challenges and unmanageable complexity that plague traditional, centralized monolithic data infrastructures.[76]

Data Fabric

While data mesh is heavily focused on organizational change, people, processes, and business domain data ownership, a new paradigm called *data fabric* is emerging to focus on technology and architecture.

According to Gartner's *Top Strategic Technology Trends* for 2022, "By 2024, data fabric deployments will quadruple efficiency in data utilization while cutting human-driven data management tasks in half."[77]

Data fabric is a design concept that offers a new way to power business applications with a network of information via a connected enterprise architecture. It uses data virtualization to provide API and connectors for integrating internal datastore silos and external third-party vendors. It is about discovering metadata assets to tackle organizational data complexity and building data products with human intervention, machine capabilities, appropriate

---

76   https://www.softlanding.ca/blog/data-mesh-a-fresh-approach-to-data-organization/

77   https://www.gartner.com/en/information-technology/insights/top-technology-trends

technical integration, architecture, and consolidation across various data environments.[78] Commercial vendors such as Data Bricks, Starburst and Informatica offer data fabric and data mesh options.

Data Federation and Virtualization

According to Denodo, "Data federation is a technology that enables two or more databases to appear as one, whether they be on-premises or in the cloud."[79] The data federation concept has been around since the 1980s. It gets rebranded and repackaged with the latest technological advancement every decade, and data fabric is its latest offshoot.

Data virtualization is a subset of data federation. It is best described as the technology that fuels data federation. Modern data virtualization vendors such as SAP HANA, Informatica, and Talend are leaders in this space.[80] They provide data abstraction, metadata repository, read-and-write query access, and processing features over a wide range of data silos and systems.

One open source technology worth noting in the Data Fabric/Federation space is Trino. Trino, which originally started as PrestoDB in the data infrastructure research labs of Meta (Facebook), is gaining popularity. Trino is not a database with storage but can be considered a virtual DW or an "on-the-fly data DW." It is an SQL query engine that uses standardized SQL queries and connectors to HDFS/Hive, MySQL, PostgreSQL, Kafka, Cassandra, Redis, and many more data stores. Trino exposes data silos at their source without the need to migrate data to a single location (*Fig. 40*)

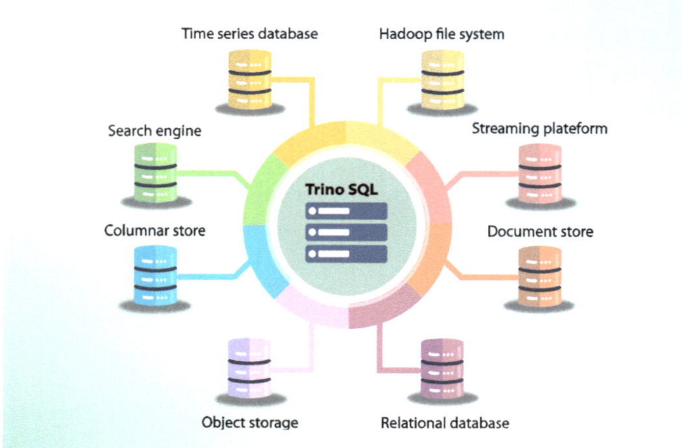

Fig. 40: Trino SQL Query Engine

---

78   https://www.jamesserra.com/archive/2021/06/data-fabric-defined/

79   https://www.denodo.com/en/data-virtualization/data-federation

80   https://www.gartner.com/reviews/market/data-virtualization

Data Hub

A data hub is a data integration pattern that serves as a wrapper around data fabric. It facilitates the sharing of enterprise application operationalized master data seamlessly across DWs and data lakes via secure API connectors.

Metadata Management

Metadata management is a valuable component of data management. Incorporating standardized formats, metadata terms, and controlled vocabulary facilitates faster and better-optimized search and retrieval capabilities. This, in turn, enables quicker responses to data requests, improved accountability, and a greater level of compliance with legal and regulatory requirements. Implementing strict data governance policies to dictate retention, privacy, compliance, and security practices around data usage prevents data lakes from becoming data swamps. With the advent of off-the-shelf master data management (MDM) software solutions and data catalogs over the last few years, managing data has become easier.

Operationalizing Data Pipelines

Operationalizing input and output data pipelines is a critical step for businesses doing advanced analytics, and its importance is typically overlooked. Rigorous data engineering—the building, operationalization, and management of data pipelines—is critical to good data management.

Organizations should thus be sure to allocate sufficient resources and funding to data pipeline development and maintenance. Avoiding siloed or ad hoc approaches to data pipeline operationalization can help shore up everything from an organization's data quality to its security, regulatory compliance, and revenues. Data pipeline management should involve a multi-functional team that includes engineers, data owners, and data stewards and other governance professionals focused on terminology alignment, standardization, security, regulatory compliance, and accessibility for all corporate data.

In some organizations, engineers may not have access to a software development environment (sandbox) or to the production data pipelines needed to build advanced analytics models. These engineers may obtain a copy or snapshot of the data stored in their departmental server, using it to generate their own production-quality data pipelines and management systems. This solution enables them to get a head start on analytics, data validation, feasibility studies, and proof-of-concept models on their local machines and—in organizations without a solid technological footing or experience in software product development—may seem a logical place to start.

Such makeshift solutions, however, undermine reliability, reproducibility, and automation, and can result in data loss and limitations in software versioning and scalability. These issues can in turn introduce system risks, resulting in loss of revenue and trust, and may discourage user adoption in future technology transformation projects. Users rejecting new technology projects may go back to their old ways and resort to using spreadsheets, reducing productivity, diminishing organizational morale, and contributing to attrition.[81]

Businesses that are hesitant to commit resources to data pipelines may place the responsibility for the pipeline feeding analytics software or operational production processes in the hands of a lone software engineer. This situation introduces points of potential failure in the company's business processes and systems. The risks engendered by this insecure pipeline can be further exacerbated by outages and process failures, resulting in revenue loss.

Data Management and Processing for Big Data and AI

Making the Case for Big Data

While relational databases work well for descriptive analytics, BI solutions, or retrospective analysis, they have severe limitations, particularly when it comes to managing the vast proliferation of unstructured data streams generated in today's digital world.

In the post–COVID-19 world, Big Data technologies are more valuable than ever, due to our heavy dependence on streaming and other online platforms and internet services that enable us to work, learn, play, and socialize from home.

Today's organizations rely on Big Data, AI, and machine learning (ML) techniques to enhance customer experience, optimize online platform performance and strengthen fault detection, to name just a few uses. In combination, Big Data technologies and ML enable the real-time collection and processing of complex customer transactions and records, thereby generating valuable insights to drive organizational and operational excellence. In addition, they help strategic corporate initiatives by enabling predictive and prescriptive analytics, or basic strategic analytics. These analytic capabilities, in turn, improve decision-making by providing actionable intelligence related to everything from growth opportunities and new markets to products to explore.

According to Statista's *Big Data and Analytics Services Global Market 2021* report, the Big Data and analytics market will grow from 76 billion dollars in 2020 to 117 billion dollars in 2025.[82] The report attributes the expected increase to the global recovery from the COVID-19 pandemic and our increasingly heavy reliance on IoT in our daily lives. Statista also forecasts that the global Big Data analytics market will hit 68 billion dollars in 2025 and ascribes that revenue growth to advanced analytics.

---

81   https://hbr.org/sponsored/2021/04/the-state-of-digital-adoption-2021
82   https://www.statista.com/statistics/254266/global-big-data-market-forecast/

The Four V's of Big Data

Since the early days of Big Data, there has been exponential growth in research and development (R&D) efforts to tackle data management challenges related to the velocity, variety, veracity, and volume (the *4 V's*) of Big Data. Big Data technologies employ large-scale computation systems that allow parallel processing, such as Apache Spark and databases such as Apache Cassandra, Apache HBase, Apache Hive, and MongoDB. Distributed computing systems like these are scalable, fault-tolerant, and cost-effective at processing and managing Big Data.[83]

Distributed Computing Frameworks

In distributed computing frameworks, components of a software system are shared among multiple computers in a network, improving efficiency and performance in large-scale data processing. Distributed computing frameworks are cost-effective because they typically run on commodity (off-the-shelf) hardware, including memory, processor and hard drive. The computers (nodes) in a distributed framework each have the exact same hardware specifications and function as one unit, in a *cluster*, working in unison to coordinate, compute and execute the data processing of workloads.

By combining their memory and processing power, the computers in the cluster increase overall performance, allowing for rapid data access and high processing speeds. Large, computationally heavy data retrieval tasks can be split into smaller tasks and task execution can be distributed across the nodes in the cluster, permitting data processing to be run in parallel (parallel processing).

Apache Spark—which is specifically designed to store, process, and analyze Big Data sets— has a cluster manager that allows the coordination of workloads across the computers (nodes) in a cluster. Data can also be stored locally on each of the nodes to allow for data locality. Spark attempts to ensure that data does not have to be shuffled between nodes. It does this by bringing the compute to the data.

Spark simplifies the preparation of large data sets and allows for seamless integration of AI workloads by enabling connection to popular frameworks such as R, Python, SciKit-Learn, Pytorch, and TensorFlow. Spark has also inspired the emergence of a growing ecosystem of third-party Spark packages (*Fig. 41*). Hence, Spark is a favorite among data scientists. While relational databases such as MySQL and PostgreSQL are here to stay, distributed computing and parallel processing are critical components of AI projects.

---

83   https://www.thebusinessresearchcompany.com/report/big-data-and-analytics-services-market-global-report-2020-30-covid-19-growth-and-change

Fig. 41: Spark ecosystem

Cloud Computing

Cloud computing refers to physical computers (servers) housed in data centers that store your data and make it accessible over the internet. Cloud computing allows on-demand metered data storage and has revolutionized AI and Big Data. The terms elastic, AI, and Big Data are used in conjunction with cloud computing because it allows organizations to adopt infrastructure as a service (IaaS), providing the flexibility to scale up or down depending on their changing needs. Microsoft Azure and AWS (Amazon Web Services) are popular cloud service providers (CSP) (*Fig. 42*).

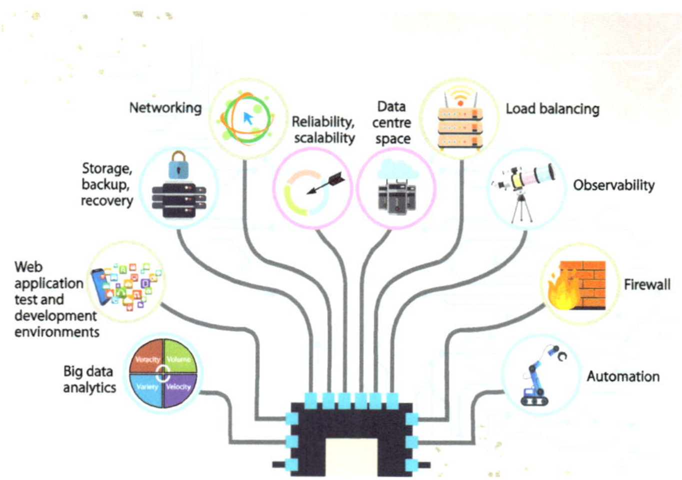

Fig. 42: Representation of infrastructure as a service (IasS)

According to a 2022 report by Gartner, 90% of new D&A deployments will be implemented through a robust UAP, causing consolidation across D&A tools by 2025.[84] The infrastructure as a service (IaaS) model provides high-performance computing (HPC). HPC architecture includes storage, network, and compute. Software programs and diverse data ingest and output pipelines are run simultaneously and seamlessly on high-compute servers that are networked in a cluster. IaaS facilitates ease of use for AI and advanced analytics workloads and can help organizations shift the upfront cost (capital expenditure or CAPEX) of on-premises infrastructure investments for database servers to the operating expenditure (OPEX) column. Hence IaaS is highly favored by business-savvy executives.

Cloud computing also allows organizations without their own analytics software capabilities to use analytics as a service (AaaS) platforms to organize, analyze and present their data. These services are relatively inexpensive and come with extensive data infrastructure, analytics hardware, and software bundles to choose from. Teradata, Databricks, Azure, AWS, Google Cloud, and Snowflake are competitors in this landscape (*Fig. 43*).

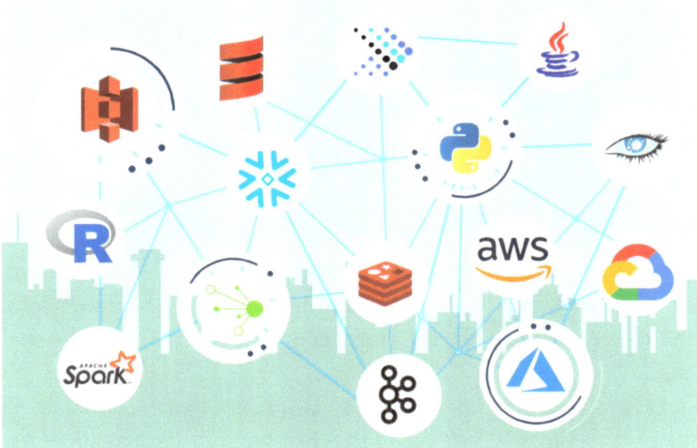

Fig. 43: Cloud analytics platforms

All cloud providers furnish the technologies that allow for advanced analytics, including ML frameworks, third-party data science tools, highly distributed persistence engines, cheap and highly durable storage, and more. These cloud providers enable advanced analytics practitioners to set up their development environment to do ML quickly. They offer the flexibility to pick their programming language of choice. R, Java, Scala, and Python programming languages are supported. They have built-in technologies to process high-volume analytics workloads and real-time streaming data, as well batch

---

84　https://www.cloudera.com/campaign/2022-gartner-magic-quadrant-for-cloud-database-management-systems/2022-gartner-magic-quadrant-for-cloud-dbms-thank-you.html?cid=7012H000001Z0PxQAK

data. Leveraging third-party cloud providers eliminates challenges with infrastructure implementation, software and hardware updates, maintenance, and associated costs. Analytics practitioners can focus on extracting business value instead of worrying about server administration and tooling maintenance.

AI Platforms

AI platforms are gaining popularity, as they provide the ability to develop applications from scratch and offer software design tools. These platforms, which can automatically convert raw data into an algorithm-friendly format, provide many built-in algorithms and their drag-and-drop capabilities make them easy to use. AWS AI services, Microsoft Azure AI, and Google Cloud AI are leaders in this space, popular due to their ease of use and ability to provide actionable insights with low-code options.[85]

To Summarize:

In this chapter, we discussed the evolution of data storage technologies, from the data warehousing of the 1980s to the Big Data technologies of the 2000s capable of handling unstructured data, to more recent distributed computing frameworks like Spark and Snowflake. We also looked at the ways organizations can use Big Data technologies to combine huge data streams in new and effective ways, thereby gaining novel perspectives, finding patterns, and deriving insights that would otherwise be missed. The profusion of low-cost data storage and management platforms that have become available in recent years have encouraged many organizations to embrace Big Data and advanced analytics, and the available options continue to multiply and evolve.

Essential Takeaways:

- Relational databases in first-generation enterprise data warehouses are limited to storing structured data, meaning that businesses must find newer solutions if they want to utilize the vast range of unstructured data generated by the Internet of Things.
- Data lakes are second-generation data repositories that can store an organization's structured data and a wide range of unprocessed, raw, unstructured data.
- Big Data technologies employ large-scale computation systems that allow parallel and distributed processing and are capable of handling high volumes of unstructured data. Open source Big Data technologies are currently popular, such as Apache Spark, Apache Cassandra, Apache HBase, Apache Hive, and MongoDB.[86]
- Cloud computing allows on-demand metered data storage and computing resources to be made accessible over the internet, enabling organizations to adopt infrastructure as a service (IaaS), which provides the flexibility to scale up or down depending on their changing needs.

---

85   https://venturebeat.com/ai/10-top-artificial-intelligence-solutions-in-2022/
86   https://www.techrepublic.com/article/data-science-skills-gap/

- A recent paradigm shift away from centralized forms of data architecture has given rise to decentralized data storage and management solutions such as data lakehouses, data mesh, and data fabric.
- Data fabric and data mesh provide an architecture to access data across multiple technologies and platforms, the key difference being, data fabric is technology-centric, while data mesh focuses on governance and organizational change.

Chapter 7

The Analytics Product Life Cycle™

On a conceptual level, the Analytics Product Life Cycle—the process of developing an advanced analytics model and its resulting analytics product (application)—can be broken into a sequence of stages and corresponding domain quadrants, each of which involves its own specific set of tasks. This step-by-step breakdown is analogous to the way the software development life cycle (SDLC) is conceptualized in the information technology (IT) management setting.

To depict the APLC graphically, we have adapted a model that represents the cross-industry standard process for data mining, explained by IBM as follows:

"CRISP-DM, which stands for Cross-Industry Standard Process for Data Mining, is an industry-proven way to guide your data mining efforts. As a methodology, it includes descriptions of the typical phases of a project, the tasks involved with each phase, and an explanation of the relationships between these tasks. As a process model, CRISP-DM provides an overview of the data mining life cycle."[87]

Here, we have broken the APLC into the following quadrants:[88]

- Business
- Data engineering
- Modeling
- Software engineering

Each APLC quadrant shows the activity associated with a particular stage in the *Analytics Product Life Cycle* (APLC) and can have up to four associated steps (*Fig. 44*).

---

87   https://www.ibm.com/docs/en/spss-modeler/SaaS?topic=dm-crisp-help-overview

88   Shearer, C. (2000) The CRISP-DM Model: The New Blueprint for Data Mining. Journal of Data Warehousing, 5, 13-22

APLC Quadrant	Stages	APLC Activities
Business	Project right sizing and problem framing	Pick a small but high-impact problem
	Evaluate culture	Evaluate analytics innovation, organizational culture
	Identify a sponsor	Find executive sponsor to influence and encourage, remove roadblocks
	Create a team	Create a multidisciplinary team
Data engineering	Data collection and management	Evaluate organizational D&A strategy, conduct data discovery, manage data acquisition and processing
Modeling	Advanced analytics modeling	Develop and refine advanced analytics models
	Validate, verify, iterate	Consult domain experts, solicit user feedback, iterate
Software engineering	Implement, test, iterate	Implement, iterate, verify, validate, feedback loops not lines
	Embedded analytics	Embed analytics product in organizational process and workflow.

Fig. 44: Analytics Product Life Cycle (APLC) activities

It is important to note here that, while the APLC can be viewed as a series of stages, it does not necessarily proceed in a strictly linear fashion. Instead, it should be seen as a set of iterative processes that can and should loop back to revisit previous steps whenever more information or a rethinking of strategy is needed.

It is also the case that the APLC can be quite variable within and across organizations, with iteration being prompted by factors specific to a business's level of Analytics Fitness and other internal factors.

In this chapter, we will learn about the APLC from start to finish, gaining a holistic view of the analytics engineering process and an overview of each quadrant (*Fig. 45*), before zeroing in on the final quadrant in greater detail in Chapter 8 (*Prototype to Analytics Product*). Throughout this chapter, you will encounter terms, concepts and nuances that will by now be familiar and you will observe how they fit together as an organization progresses through the essential steps in the APLC.

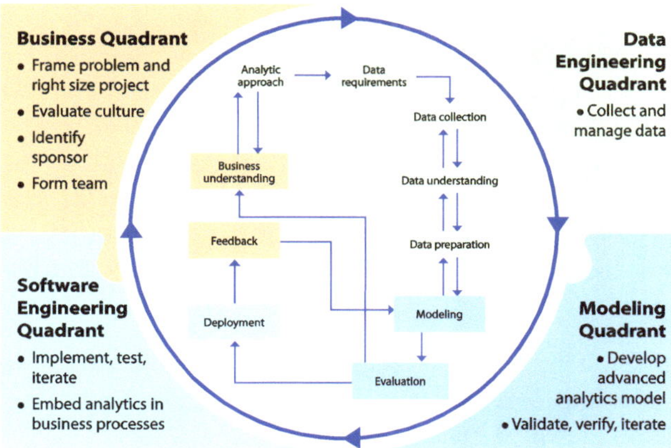

Fig. 45: Analytics Product Life Cycle (APLC) quadrants

As we progress through the stages of the APLC, we will focus on advanced analytics end-to-end workflow rather than descriptive analytics. Some of the guiding principles outlined here, however, can be applied to descriptive analytics and BI projects as well, which will be covered in detail in future volumes of this book or in blog posts by this author.

Business Quadrant

The business quadrant is the first stage in the APLC, in which the project team tackles the tasks of project right sizing and problem framing. We delved into many of the concepts and challenges associated with this stage in Chapter 4 (*The Analytics Triad™: Goals, Metrics, Data & Analytics Strategy*), when we discussed goal setting and defining a D&A strategy. We will now provide a holistic view of the way the decisions and actions in the business quadrant of the APLC fit together in a series of practical steps, in the context of an advanced analytics project. (*Fig. 46*).

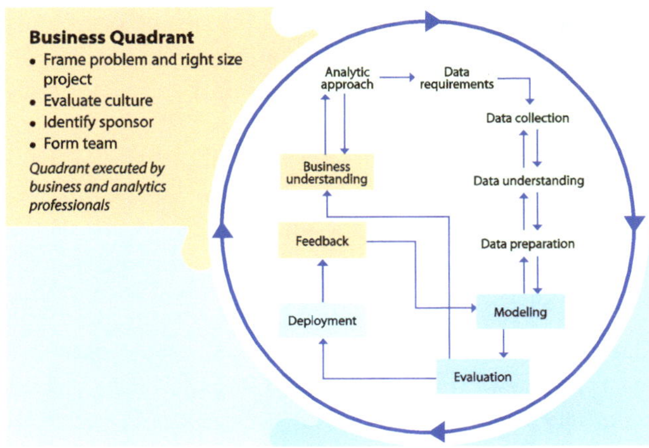

Fig. 46: Business quadrant – Analytics Product Life Cycle (APLC)

Choose a Small But High-Impact Problem

Analytics project right sizing requires careful deliberation. The chosen project should be impactful enough to generate results that build organizational enthusiasm but small enough to get off the ground quickly without requiring either elaborate architecture or the support of a large department. This does not mean that one should start the exercise with whatever datasets are available. The desired business outcomes and the criteria for project success must be clearly defined. All those involved in the project must be cognizant of its goal, which may be focused on anything from finding growth drivers to reducing process bottlenecks.

The business problem at the core of the project must be clearly defined and used as the basis for the creation of a data acquisition, management, and manipulation blueprint, or D&A strategy. The following are key factors to consider:

- Business value-chain proposition
- Project outcome measurements
- Impact on existing processes
- Whether the goal is a large-scale organizational process improvement vs. a change that affects only a limited set of users
- Timeline of delivery and deployment
- Software, hardware, data, and technology dependencies and resource availability

The list above is not meant to be exhaustive but instead outlines the fundamental factors that must be considered in the business quadrant of the APLC. Each organization will have its own unique circumstances and considerations that must be factored into this phase.

Frame the Problem

Once a tightly defined, highly impactful problem of reasonable scope has been chosen, the next step involves writing a business problem statement. The business problem statement is a succinct, relevant, unambiguous description of the business objective and organizational goals the project aims to achieve. It is written in business terms. In the best case scenario, a department head or executive seeking the services of the advanced analytics team will generate the business problem statement, ideally in consultation with the analytics team. The latter will provide practical insight into problem right sizing and feasibility given the organization's technical resources and available expertise. Setting down a clear business problem statement that begins with the business team is a critical first step that will kick off the APLC on the right foot and ensure that team business and team analytics are united in pursuing a clear, shared goal.

Unfortunately, due to many of the structural, cultural and communication factors that we have discussed in the previous chapters, this ideal scenario rarely happens. Instead, the business problem or statement will likely have to be created from scratch by the advanced analytics team, in collaboration with the executive sponsor and the business domain subject matter expert (SME).

Nelson P. Reppening, Don Kieffer and Todd Astor, writing in the Spring 2017 issue of the *MIT Sloan Management Review*, provide a simple recipe for generating a good problem statement. Although not explicitly written for senior executives and advanced analytics practitioners leading organizational, analytical digital transformations, their statement outlines valuable concepts that can provide a foundation for business problem framing in the analytics context:

> *There are few management skills more powerful than the discipline of clearly articulating the problem you seek to solve before jumping into action. A good problem statement has five basic elements:*
> - *It references something the organization cares about and connects that element to a clear and specific goal;*
> - *it contains a clear articulation of the gap between the current state and the goal;*
> - *the key variables—the target, the current state, and the gap—are quantifiable;*
> - *it is as neutral as possible concerning possible diagnoses or solutions; and*
> - *it is sufficiently small in scope that you can tackle it quickly.*[89]

Accurately framing the problem at hand helps the advanced analytics team appreciate the intricacies of the business processes in need of remediation. They can then appropriately prioritize project needs. A clear problem statement enables the team to ask specific questions, identify potential obstacles or bottlenecks, and help refresh or reframe the project goals, if necessary for technical reasons.

Of course, technology and business strategy are interdependent factors in any analytics project, with technological limitations or advances either limiting or expanding the realistic scope of the business strategy envisioned by the project team. According to a 2022 research survey conducted by management consulting firm KPMG, 66% of organizations have been very or extremely effective in using digital technology transformation to advance business strategy.[90] A clear problem statement must therefore reflect the organization's current business priorities and digital technology capabilities.

A clearly defined problem statement will help the project team find direct, cost-effective ways to reach its goals. It will prevent the team from later having to spin off additional projects to capture variables not included in the initial brief, or from being sidetracked by a search for out-of-scope solutions to issues not relevant to the central business problem. Problem framing propels the articulation of optimal business use cases, proof of concept (POC), project scoping, and potential phased pilot-to-production approaches.

An adept framing of the business problem enables the advanced analytics team to focus on relevant project discovery and data availability, and to determine project feasibility. In software engineering projects, analysts, program managers, or product managers are

---

89   https://sloanreview.mit.edu/article/the-most-underrated-skill-in-management/

90   https://advisory.kpmg.us/articles/2022/2022-us-technology-survey.html?utm_source=vanity&utm_
      medium=ref

responsible for gathering project requirements and creating the software development product design. A well-defined business problem statement will ensure that the project's steps and processes are streamlined and clear to those responsible for them.

In advanced analytics projects, the parameters of the business problem statement will be profoundly impacted by the analytics methodologies and technologies used to execute it. It is thus critical that problem framing in the advanced analytics context be conducted in collaboration with a senior advanced analytics architect who can provide expert insight into the analytics architecture and data issues. Given that the execution of an analytics project depends on a relatively scarce resource—the seasoned analytics engineer (or engineers)—it is all the more important that the central problem be well-defined, to avoid squandering the engineer's limited time.

A clearly defined business problem statement is also vital because it can generate a formal business use case and create budget justification for additional resources, infrastructure or platform investment, tools, or training. The business use case can also assist in framing business metrics and KPIs for assessment of the results generated by the analytics project. In all, a good problem statement affords an accurate evaluation of the parameters of the project, facilitates investment, and helps win organizational approval before the hands-on technical project kick-off.

Return on investment (ROI) is a topic that often surfaces when generating a business use case or justification for investment in resources. In advanced analytics, this is a complicated subject to tackle.

Since advanced analytics projects are complex, converting the value gained from them into accurate, justifiable numbers is not a straightforward undertaking. As we saw in Chapter 2 (*Why Link Analytics and Business?*), predictive and prescriptive analytics efforts are capable of unearthing unforeseen insights that can not necessarily be guessed at when establishing business use cases at the outset of a project. This fact makes it difficult to lay out a business justification that anticipates the project's outcomes.

If an advanced analytics project is executed well, however, it will likely result in significant gains in operational process advancements and innovation. With the benefit of perspective, it will be clear that advanced analytics provides insights and business guidance that cannot be obtained in any other way; hence its value is incomparable. Project gains will be high, likely outweighing infrastructure investments or cloud service provider (CSP) expenditure. These gains, however, may be intangible and holistic at the outset. The support of technologically savvy management may be needed to rationalize the initial investment and get the first advanced analytics projects off the ground.

Define Success

Gaining a quantitative measurement of return on investment (ROI) is typically difficult to accomplish in the early stages of analytics projects. A suitable alternative can be outlining key advantages and possible positive outcomes of successful projects.

At the very least, an advanced analytics project should:

- Provide a comprehensive overview of operations
- Integrate data sources and reduce manual data munging for improved automated data preparation in the future
- Automate data acquisition and manipulation for modeling workflows
- Keep the data and software auditable and reusable
- Uncover avenues for business metrics to be measured and monitored
- Incrementally add more data and advanced analytics features to the organization's existing data architecture
- Provide results that are formatted for ease of use, especially by non-technical employees
- Accelerate business decision-making and work prioritization
- Simplify operational processes, reduce manual workflows, and enhance productivity
- Create shared organizational expertise with reusable D&A software
- Facilitate gradual organizational restructuring to avoid culture shock
- Create a valuable asset and pave the way for innovation

Evaluate Organizational Culture

Getting started on a new advanced analytics project is akin to conducting research or experimentation in any scientific discipline. The analytics teams will explore, experiment with new ideas, perhaps examine data from uncharted business functions, and combine state-of-the-art technologies and algorithms to accelerate learning and derive results.

Some businesses may be built upon mechanistic organizational foundations, with rigidly demarcated departments. In such organizations, control and command are tightly managed by the top echelons of management and decision-making is done in a centralized fashion by a few who may not have a good read on what is happening on the front lines.

When initiating organizational analytics transformation projects, the following goals should be central to the planning process:

- providing widespread data access via data democratization
- creating a culture of transparency and knowledge dissemination
- upskilling employees
- offering easy-to-use unified analytics platforms (UAP) with intuitive user interfaces (UI)

If these objectives are implemented iteratively and successfully achieved, they will nudge the organization toward becoming more collaborative and primed for future analytics projects. These changes will allow the organization's analytics technology culture to shift. This shift, in turn, will ideally facilitate the alignment of organizational goals and create a sense of shared ownership of both success and failure across departments and levels, generating additional feedback loops between frontline workers and management, and creating a more engaged workforce and quicker decision-to-action cycles.

In practice, however, this desirable outcome may not be easy to achieve, as the selection of an organization's inaugural analytics project can also be a very contentious process and there are a number of possible cultural obstacles that may block or hinder a paradigm shift in the direction of data democratization.

We discussed many of these internal roadblocks throughout the previous chapters, including the impenetrability of some business silos, as well as human foibles related to competition, territoriality, and control. Opposing aspirations, conflicting work ethics, operational inertia, premeditated resistance, or risk aversion are all challenges that can arise. The paradigm shift wrought by analytics and automation may be felt as an imminent threat to employee tenure and—in the absence of adequate upskilling or change management initiatives— may alienate those missing analytical skill sets and competencies, ultimately resulting in attempts to block projects.

Some organizations may not have an innovative culture at the outset and may therefore be unreceptive to data democratization. It is also sometimes the case that previously innovative companies that have succumbed to market pressure and resorted to procuring innovative start-ups to keep up with market trends may become resistant to pursuing organic analytics innovation or investing in advanced analytics efforts in situ.

So, how can we overcome these obstacles and make progress?

Identify a Sponsor

Why does every analytics project need a sponsor? Some of the challenges we discussed in the previous section can be diminished by engaging a technology-savvy executive sponsor early in the APLC. The sponsor plays a cardinal role in fostering a culture of innovation, encouraging exploration and experimentation, removing roadblocks, and buffering failures during the APLC. Rigorous knowledge of specific operations, policies, and architectures is not required to function as a sponsor, but interpersonal competencies and the ability to influence are necessary.

The sponsor should commit time to the project, work effectively with the analytics team, and resolve conflicts, if necessary. The sponsor should be engaged throughout the APLC and be committed to the project goals. Why? Analytics digital transformation projects have a higher likelihood of success and a propensity to take hold when savvy executives can procure funding, obtain quick wins, and celebrate them with compelling stories to mobilize the workforce over the span of the project. Further, a sponsor can smooth the way for the project team, removing internal roadblocks the team may encounter. Sponsors provide cover from organizational politics and communicate successes and challenges to senior management, playing a crucial role in securing the resources and support needed to complete the project.

An analytics project, if successful, may reveal important business insights. It may also shed light on inefficiencies in existing processes and create transparency about suboptimal group performance, uncovering facts that may not be welcome or appreciated by all. When a project disrupts conventional thinking, project teams may face challenging obstacles. In these situations, the role of the sponsor in buffering the analytics team from organizational backlash is vitally important.

Create a Multidisciplinary Project Team

So how do you staff an advanced analytics project? Do you just hire the mythical unicorn "full- stack" data scientist who has become the stuff of legend?[91] The answer is no. Allocating only one engineering resource to tackle end-to-end analytics development and production deployment is inadvisable. It is one of the sure-shot ways of setting up an analytics project to fail.

It is imperative to recruit team members whose skills are drawn from diverse functional departments. Ideally, these individuals will be unbiased, curious lifelong learners who possess intellectual bravery: so-called trailblazers and "risk takers." (*Fig. 47*)

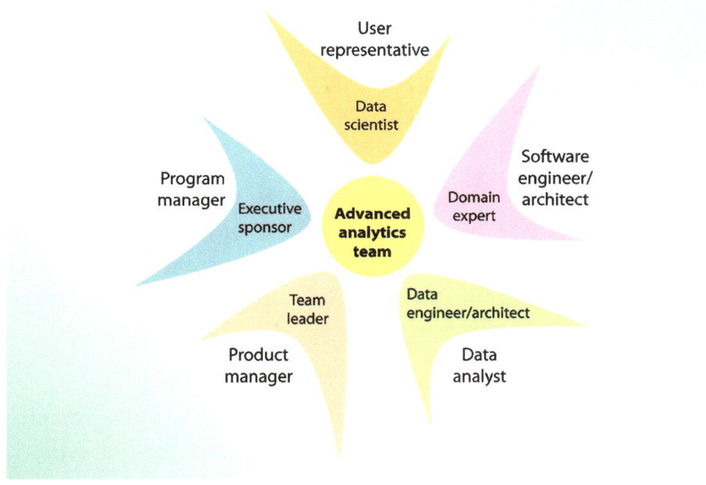

Fig. 47: Advanced analytics team

In addition to individuals with data science, software engineering, data engineering, application, and data architecture skills, the project team should include experts from various other activity spheres, such as product managers, program managers, software quality engineers, architects, data stewards, and analysts with non-overlapping skill sets. The size of this multifunctional group will depend upon the complexity of the project, the size of the organization, and the kinds of resources that are obtainable.

---

91   https://www.tomdavenport.com/beyond-unicorns-educating-classifying-and-certifying-business-data-scientists/

Domain Experts

Typically, a domain expert has in-depth knowledge of the business problem or processes being investigated and can steer the project in the right direction. Domain experts may be product managers, aspiring managers, or engineers. Domain experts possess extensive knowledge about specific operations, technologies, or challenges pertaining to markets, customers, processes, competitors, production, finance, or vertical business functions. They can potentially convince senior management of the validity of the ideas and the value the analytics project brings to the business. They tend to work with more technically inclined engineers and can vouch for the feasibility of new ideas.

Advanced Analytics Practitioners

As we saw in Chapter 5 (*Linking Analytics to Business: Roles, Expertise and Organizational Culture*), businesses are pulling out all the stops to hire skilled analytics polymaths, and are using a slew of approaches to identify potential analytics team members who are exceptional at ideation. Doctorate degrees, experience in advanced analytics techniques and technology, a collaborative mindset, and native intelligence are highly sought-after attributes. While these qualities are critical, practitioners should ideally also have strong interpersonal skills, a knack for gathering information from a variety of people and sources, the ability to break down artificial constructs promoted by cliques within an organization, and the insight needed to navigate and dismantle structured organizational silos.

The ideal advanced analytics practitioner can go beyond the strictures imposed by organizational hierarchies and boundaries to access information. They can abstract concepts from a deluge of information derived from diverse sources. They can synthesize information from one product or team to develop a novel product or concept for another team. They possess an entrepreneurial spirit and occupy brokerage positions in organizational networks.

Furthermore, they possess strong technical and quantitative skills, comprehend data flows, have rigorous training in experimental design, and recognize the underlying assumptions they use in their algorithmic logic. They have expertise in advanced analytics and statistical techniques, as well as in business consulting skills, and they maintain an open-minded approach. They have prior experience or are willing to find ways to keep up to date with state-of-the-art database technologies, cloud computing, and associated analytics platforms. Depending on the size of the organization, these engineers may need to pinch hit and serve functions ordinarily performed in a variety of roles: database administrator (DBA), data engineer, data scientist, ML engineer, architect, cybersecurity expert, cloud storage and software-as-a-service (SaaS) aficionado, AI guru, statistical modeler, software engineer, deep learning pundit, and user interface (UI) and user experience designer.

Team Leader

The team leader is usually an engineer from the multifunctional collaborative team formed to execute the analytics project—someone fellow engineers and management trust to see the project to completion. In larger organizations, this engineer may be borrowed for a specific time from an experienced centralized analytics team or functional group. An organization may also have program managers working closely with the designated team leader to keep projects on track, communicate results and challenges, and remove roadblocks for engineers or projects in general.

It is the role of the team leader to function as a conduit between the executive leadership, the sponsor, and the engineers; share results; create architectural diagrams; make design decisions; share milestones; identify risks; and negotiate and reduce conflicts. A team leader must speak both the relevant technical language and the business language to ensure that the technical implementation produces the expected business outcomes.

User Representative

The team should include a representative from the user community for which the analytics software is being built. The user representative understands the inner workings of the business, possesses strong interpersonal skills, is business savvy, and can be a change agent for any adjustments to organizational processes that are needed based on insights uncovered by the analytics project. The user representative works closely with the engineering team leader, reviews progress, provides feedback and approval, and is instrumental in implementing the results of the analytics project.

For example, an analytics project for a sales department may uncover new avenues to reduce costs or increase revenue that go against the grain of the department's existing culture or incentive structure. In a *"we have always done it this way"* culture, a commitment from the user community's department head to be responsive in addressing process inefficiencies uncovered by the analytics project may need to be obtained even before the start of the project. This commitment should be reinforced by the project's sponsor.

As outlined in Chapter 4 (*The Analytics Triad™: Goals, Metrics, and Data & Analytics Strategy*), identifying how the data will be used and what business questions need to be answered is a critical component of the groundwork needed for a D&A project. It is therefore crucial that the organization assemble a collaborative, multidisciplinary team to delineate project strategy.

Data Engineering Quadrant

Data engineering *(Fig. 48)* can be defined as:

Building, managing and operationalizing data pipelines in support of various analytics demands (for example, logical data warehouse, reporting, business intelligence [BI], advanced analytics, and AI use cases) by following defined architectural patterns, tools and methodologies.

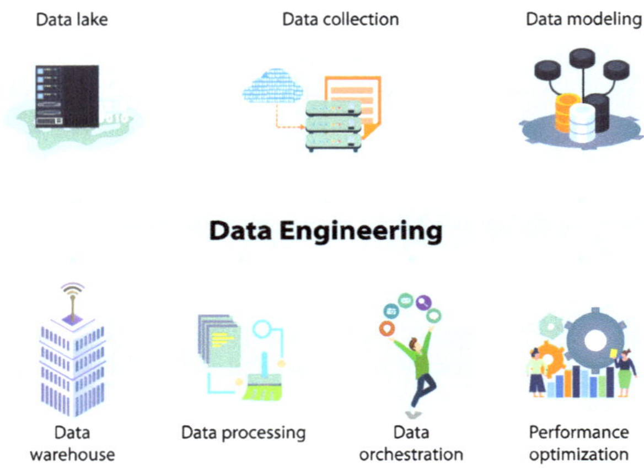

Fig. 48: Data engineering segments

The critical steps in the data engineering quadrant (*Fig. 49*) involve data discovery, data collection, and processing, as listed below.

Data discovery:

- Evaluate D&A strategy
- Identify data sources
- Evaluate data quality

Data collection and processing:

- Merge data from various data streams
- Create new variables
- Identify outliers and fill in missing values

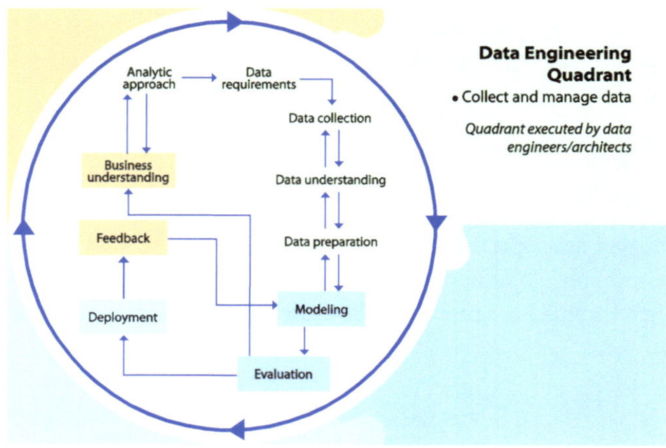

Fig. 49: Data engineering quadrant – Analytics Product Life Cycle (APLC)

Data Discovery

Evaluate Data and Analytics Strategy

The data discovery process starts with a D&A strategy evaluation. At the start of the project, the team will have examined how the analytics project strategy fits into the organization's goals and vision. As we have discussed, without this step, the analytics project may end up as a hobby project or merely an exercise in intellectual curiosity, serving a limited set of people and ultimately having little impact on the business or its decision-making processes.

In the data engineering quadrant, the project team must delve more deeply into the analytics project strategy and determine a data collection and storage plan that supports the business functions the project is intended to fulfill. Unfortunately, analytics frameworks are not turn-key solutions yet. For analytics to offer business value, data acquisition and data management must be done according to a carefully defined strategy. Sound data management practices must be implemented early on and considerable thought must be given to procuring and maintaining top-quality data storage solutions.

Identify Data Sources and Evaluate Quality

Once the business problem statement is well defined, the data sources required for the project can be identified and assessed. The collaborative project team will work together to appraise data availability, provenance, and pedigree. The team members will examine the organization's data as a whole, identify data that can be leveraged as an asset, and work to reduce associated risks.

As we have discussed in previous chapters, organizations in the early stages of their analytics journey may not have a unified analytics platform (UAP) or a data warehouse (DW) or data lake where all their organizational data is stored. Instead, data may be stored in certain business pockets available to only a limited set of users. In organizations without mature data governance policies, it may be difficult to find and access data held in these organizational data silos. "Out of the box" thinking may be required to overcome organizational hurdles of this kind. To bypass these obstacles, engineers may opt to collect their data from local departmental servers. While this recourse solves the short-term problem of gaining timely access to data, it introduces risk due to the absence of backups and failover and exacerbates data governance challenges down the line.

Data Collection and Processing

Merge Data and Create New Variables

Once the requisite data sources have been pinpointed and evaluated through data discovery, work will be required to ensure that they are in the appropriate format and that their development environment can be reached by the engineers focused on modeling and data management for the project. This is the stage where organizational policies for data governance, application access, firewall rules, and security may be a potential roadblock and will need to be factored in. The semantics of the incoming data will need to be documented and rules established that specify whether a datum is valid or not. The end result of the data manipulation (processing) and preprocessing step will be contingent on user community requirements.

The advanced analytics engineers engaged in the project will extract unformatted data from various data streams, process and manipulate it, and create new variables or build suitable algorithm logic. In descriptive analytics projects, by contrast, engineers focused on data management solutions for visualization and reporting will employ statistics, labeling, and classification techniques to summarize the data pipelines into built-in formats dictated by the user community. Whether the project involves descriptive analytics or advanced analytics, this process is an essential step in the APLC. If designed and executed well, this step will alleviate many of the challenges associated with analytics project adoption and expedite the discovery of new knowledge and the dissemination of relevant organizational information.

Reevaluate and Reconcile Data: Data Wrangling

Poorly maintained, outdated, low-quality data inputs feeding downstream descriptive and advanced analytics projects will undoubtedly produce low-quality results. It is therefore essential to clean and process the data and ensure that it is in a form that can be consumed directly by mathematical models in the modeling quadrant of the APLC. Checking for erroneous data, clarifying assumptions, removing outliers, and inputting missing data are vital steps that enable an analytics team to be confident in the underlying information that will be fed into the analytics model. Converting raw data into numerical measurements (features), reducing the number of features, eliminating superfluous information, and extracting key characteristics to feed as inputs into the model are all part of this process of data wrangling for advanced analytics models and these steps must be automated to ensure that the models are built on clean data.

To create a new metric, one may have merged and aggregated data from various data sources, sets, and tables. Merging data from different sources within a single organization will involve tackling data fields and values that mean different things in disparate tables, as most organizational silos have their own business vernacular and vocabulary. In the wake of a merger and acquisition or the integration of a subsidiary, there will be additional challenges involved in achieving a unified view of customer data.

In the retail industry, for example, challenges may include merging and integrating data from customer purchases, contracts, and loyalty programs into a master customer data management system to deliver a UAP for customer experience. In the healthcare industry, organizations will need to standardize the way particular diseases and symptoms are coded in electronic health records (EHR). Without this step, the same condition might not be coded the same way by two originators and the discrepancies that arise across separate entries in a database will cause challenges during analysis.

In a study published by Tadhg Nagle and colleagues in *Harvard Business Review* in 2017, survey respondents reported that 47% of newly created data collection pipelines have at least one critical error and only 3% obtained acceptable data quality scores.[92] Thomas Davenport observes that "all work is plagued by bad data," noting that organizations waste a significant amount of time and money (resources that are often not accounted for) on fixing it."[93]

This problem can affect every facet of an organization. In a business, the sales vertical may have to spend time and money correcting data errors introduced from the marketing vertical, or the finance group may be forced to spend 75% of its resources on the alignment and collation of reports. And when executives have no confidence in the organizational metrics presented to them by fellow executives or subordinates, they may waste resources spinning off their own initiatives. Data reconciliation is therefore an important step in ensuring high-quality data for both descriptive and advanced analytics workloads.

As we discussed in Chapter 5 (*Linking Analytics to Business: Roles, Expertise and Organizational Culture*), 80–95% of an advanced analytics engineer's time is generally spent on data discovery, data wrangling and reconciliation efforts, leaving precious little time for doing the valuable work of building ML models and developing data products.

It is therefore critical that organizations allocate sufficient time and resources to data cleansing and reconciliation before data is loaded into a database, ensuring that the correct values and field description semantics are used. At this stage, it is beneficial to enlist the help of a DataDevOps team, which focuses on automated data collection, modeling, collation, processing, orchestration, quality checks, validity, completeness, performance, efficiency, accuracy, privacy, security, technological advancements, accessibility, and retention policies. It is critical to ensure that the data inputs to the advanced analytics models meet exceptional data quality standards.

Most data quality issues are caused by an organization's failure to apply pre-defined business validation rules to data creation and processes.[94] Some errors may be due to data being entered manually (free-flow text) instead of through standardized forms, dropdowns, or pre-built templates. Creating good quality validation at the source can save thousands of person-hours that would otherwise be spent fixing downstream data errors.

Information as simple as a customer name, purchase date, and phone number can take various forms, as illustrated by the following combination of entries:

- Possible variations in customer names:
    - Customer Name: I am Customer; I am Customer, Inc; Iam Customer, Pvt. Ltd.; Customer, Iam

---

92   https://www.sisense.com/embedded-pdf/?filename=https://cdn.sisense.com/wp-content/uploads/CRE1670_HBR_PS_Sisense_March2021-1.pdf

93   https://www.tomdavenport.com/getting-serious-about-data-and-data-science/

94   https://hbr.org/2020/02/to-improve-data-quality-start-at-the-sourc

- Possible variations in date fields:
  - Date: 1/12/2022; 12/1/2022; Jan 1, 2022, 1st Jan 2022
- Possible variations in telephone format:
  - Phone: 617-867-5309; 617867-5309,1-617867-5309

Problems can also arise when inconsistent formatting is applied to fields—for example, a field designating account names may appear as "account name," "AccountName," or "Account_Name"—and when business silos incorporate their own standards and metrics definitions.

Listed below are a few standard data checks that can resolve data quality issues. This is not intended to be a complete list. The kinds of errors one may observe may be specific to their domain area and a combination of extensive domain experience and data expertise may be required to spot most of them.

- *Outliers*
  Outliers are data values that may need to be removed because they lie outside the range being investigated in the dataset. In some cases, however, the anomalies themselves are the focus of an application, e.g., when the goal is to detect behavior such as fraudulent credit transactions or security violations.

- *Deduplication*
  In deduplication, extraneous and redundant data is removed from the dataset.

- *Terminology and Logic of Data Column Fields*
  Consistent terminology and logic should be applied to the data column fields used both within and across business verticals. Siloed business verticals may develop their own definitions to describe the fields they use and may also apply their own statistical methods and logic to arrive at the field values they typically employ.

  A customer billing database, for example, may have a "Customer" field used to designate current customers, defined as customers who have purchased a product in the last 30 days. Within the same organization, a customer loyalty database, on the other hand, may define a current customer as one that has made a purchase within the past 120 days.

- *Data Staleness*
  Data should be kept current and maintained using a scheduled update cycle, and historical data should be stored and archived according to organizational guidelines.

- *Conversion Tables*
  Variations across measurement systems should be resolved, e.g., between System International (SI) measurements vs. non-metric systems in the US.

Getting the whole organization aligned on terminology, fields, and metrics definitions will simplify the workload for analytics professionals and reduce confusion in interpreting results.

A unified analytics platform (UAP), where massive data streams are collated via ETL (or ELT), and subject to data quality checks, can govern the transfer of data from a source system to a target system, making valuable information easily accessible and removing data quality hurdles. The availability of data profiling tools that investigate data duplication, data accuracy, data completeness, and other data quality issues has also made it easier to resolve some of these issues quickly. Data scrubbing before loading tables in a database is possible with the help of data profiling software provided by companies such as Oracle, IBM, Talend, and SAS. However, not all issues can be resolved by using data profiling tools. A combination of established validation and verification methods, domain expertise, and organizational tribal knowledge may be required to address and resolve taxing data quality issues.

Modeling Quadrant

The modeling quadrant (*Fig. 50*) is the fundamental unit in an advanced analytics project. In this stage, the advanced analytics engineers undertake the arduous process of *model development*, in which they work to translate a real-world system into mathematical relations by learning, extracting hidden patterns, and synthesizing relationships or trends in the data into a model.

The real-world systems embodied in analytics models can take many forms. In sentiment analysis, for example, user text data can be mined from social media sites and natural language processing (NLP) can be used to categorize the written language as positive, negative, or neutral, enabling companies to determine whether a product or service they offer is well received. This form of modeling can also be used for customer relationship monitoring, competitive positioning, branding, product launches, testing new markets, or campaigns.

In route optimization, a prediction algorithm considers traffic congestion, number of driving lanes, road size, bottlenecks, number of rotaries, and speed limits as inputs and presents the fastest way to reach a given destination and the expected arrival time. In the product delivery segment of the supply chain management (SCM) industry for e-commerce companies, route optimization can be used in combination with other factors, such as windows of delivery time; number of packages, drivers, and vehicles; fuel efficiency; and traffic congestion.

Analytics models can reduce uncertainty, boost reliability, and streamline operations across the supply chain and in numerous other areas.

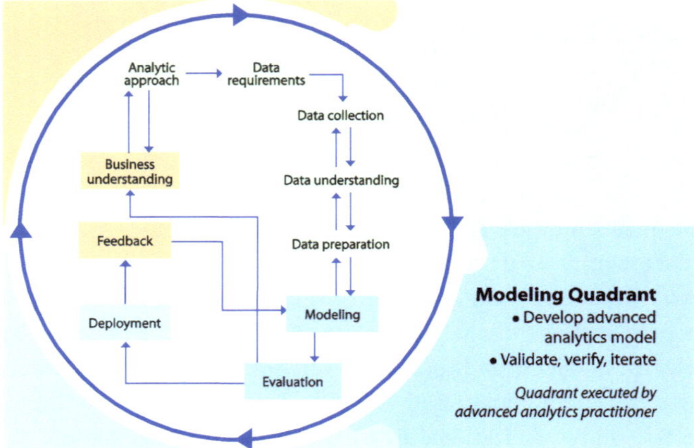

Fig. 50: Modeling quadrant – Analytics Product Life Cycle (APLC)

Develop Advanced Analytics Model

Model development is a technically sophisticated, time-consuming and often costly process that requires the incorporation of complex business logic into algorithms that identify patterns, catalog data, and transform it into a structured data type. Advanced analytics practitioners must find the algorithms and data sets that best fit the business problem at hand. They then spend weeks to months building and fine-tuning their models in the proof of concept (POC) stage. There are no cheat sheets for model-building; it takes years of experience, intuition, scientific experimentation, research acumen, and familiarity with the data—and a heavy dose of patience. Nor does the process come with any absolute guarantee of success.

According to Gartner's analysis of top strategic technology trends for 2021, "only 53% of projects make it from artificial intelligence (AI) prototypes to production."[95] This statistic is perhaps not surprising when one considers the complexity and inherent uncertainty ingrained in the process of model development. As famous statistician George Box observes, "Most models are wrong, some are useful."[96] It makes sense that advanced analytics, which is often referred to as "intangible analytics," or "strategic analytics," has an inherently lower rate of project completion than descriptive analytics, which can also be referred to as "tangible analytics."

The descriptive analytics or BI project life cycle is a relatively straightforward undertaking that takes a shorter time to complete because it has simpler goals and relies on preprocessed data that is conveniently accessible in tables that apply relevant business knowledge

---

95   https://www.gartner.com/en/newsroom/press-releases/2020-10-19-gartner-identifies-the-top-
      strategic-technology-trends-for-2021
96   https://en.wikipedia.org/wiki/All_models_are_wrong

and logic. Its outcome and results fall within an expected frame of reference and are comparatively easy to visualize and assess.

The goal of advanced analytics model-building, by contrast, is to uncover or learn something you did not know before, generating insights, making predictions, prescribing solutions, and verifying assumptions. Whether advanced analytics modeling is focused on examining historical behaviors, mimicking real-world scenarios, or optimizing complex processes, it can ultimately yield predictive and prescriptive insights capable of revolutionizing industries. It is a longer and more uncertain process than descriptive analytics, but with its risks can come high rewards.

Organizations wishing to undergo analytics transformation would be shortsighted to content themselves solely with the low hanging fruit of descriptive analytics projects. After all, a golden nugget is harder to mine than zinc, but much more valuable.

Verify and Validate

Verification and validation are critical steps in the modeling quadrant. Whether an organization is using off-the-shelf solutions or relying on back-end engineers to write advanced analytics software, the verification and validation steps of a project should not be neglected or ignored. These steps can be performed with the input of domain experts and the user community. Multiple cycles of feedback, software iteration, and new data incorporation may be required to get a good grasp of the analytics system. Whether the members of the user community will adopt and use the analytics software supplied to them depends, in part, on how involved and included they are in the data gathering, usability, validation, feedback, and iteration cycle.

In the *model evaluation* phase, there is a heavy focus on the technical quality of the model. Beyond the math, statistics, accuracy, and performance measurements embedded in the model-building process, it is necessary to connect the advanced analytics model's results back to the original project goal or business problem and assess its efficacy. This step consists of verifying and validating data input, model output, usage, and chosen metrics. The model's assumptions should also be evaluated by the organization's architects who have tribal knowledge of its systems and processes. This is the stage in which the costs associated with data storage and model compute price are weighed against business outcomes. At this point, an organization will also assess the change management process required to facilitate the operationalization of the analytics model and will quantify the project's potential return on investment.

At times, advanced analytics projects may report a metric without fully highlighting its significance or whether it has a quantifiable impact on the business process. It may not be clear why the metric is essential or whether it is the right metric to pursue. These kinds of issues are likely not a result of failures on the part of the advanced analytics team but instead a reflection of where the organization is in its analytics evolution, and the state of its own internal cohesion and management.

Mature analytics organizations have D&A verification and validation governance policies akin to or perhaps more rigorous than their software engineering best practices.

"Loops, Not Lines": Iterate and Repeat

Iteration is an essential component of advanced analytics projects. It can and should occur at any point in the modeling quadrant. Models are only as good as the approximations, assumptions, biases, heuristics, and pertinent information introduced in the process of building them. If the assumptions or conditions underlying the models change, the prediction models will need to be updated.

During the advanced analytics model-building stage, the analytics engineers may determine that the data collected and curated up to that point is unsuitable or of poor quality. This may mean that new data collection or additional research should be done—or that the team should go back to the drawing board and rethink the project's logic and data assumptions.

As we have seen above, the model evaluation phase may reveal that the model output does not adequately address the original goal or business problem underpinning the analytics project, also raising questions over project cost. Or the model evaluation process may prompt the realization that the project has been founded upon a poorly formed business question and that it is necessary to start over from scratch.

For these reasons and many others, the APLC is not necessarily a linear process that follows a rigid sequential order. Iterating—circling back to a previous step in the APLC to refine or modify a project's strategy or data—is a fundamental part of analytics product development. *"Loops, not lines,"* is the mantra to keep in mind.

When embarking upon an advanced analytics project, a useful rule of thumb is to *start small, build prototypes, iterate, and make rapid incremental advances.* This approach enables experimental, exploratory ideas to emerge, and to disappear when expendable. It is useful to roll out new analytics products incrementally to the user community, instead of launching multiple projects bundled together in a massive all-in-one rollout. Engaging users and domain experts in verification and validation during the analysis stage of the analytics project minimizes faulty business logic, erroneous data assumptions, and missed opportunities, and captures new developments in the rapidly evolving business landscape.

Software Engineering Quadrant

The software engineering stage of the APLC (*Fig. 51*) involves implementing, deploying and automating the prototype built in the modeling quadrant. We will cover this process in depth in Chapter 8 (*Prototype to Analytics Product*).

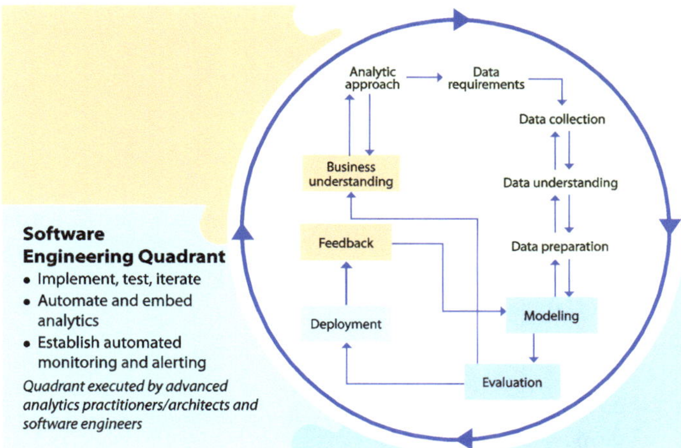

Fig. 51: Software engineering quadrant – Analytics Product Life Cycle (APLC)

Once the results of the product are initially automated, verified, and validated, it is essential to set up an automatic monitoring system that continues to check the validity of the results produced over time. It is also important to continue re-validating the assumptions underlying the product and re-testing the hypothesis over time, to assimilate revised strategy and newly available data, including data on customer behaviors. It is beneficial to provide users with an automated monitoring and alerting mechanism to flag anomalous behavior and erroneous results, either in the original data sources or in the summarized results. Doing so will increase user adoption and develop community trust in the analytics system you have developed and produced.

Embedding advanced analytics in existing organizational workflows and facilitating user adoption is its own challenge, requiring rigorous development operations (DevOps) and change management processes. We will go into this process in depth in Chapter 8 (*Prototype to Analytics Product*).

To Summarize:

The *Analytics Product Life Cycle* (APLC) can be broken into four quadrants, each with its own stages and tasks. Moving through these quadrants takes us from problem framing to forming a team, data discovery, data integration, data orchestration, and model-building, to assimilating the results produced at multiple endpoints. The advanced analytics model-building process does not follow a rigid sequential order but instead involves constant testing, refinement, updating, and even remodeling, as the model is developed and integrated into organizational workflows. Loops, *not lines*, is the mantra to remember. The vital sequence of iteration, verification and validation can occur at any stage of the APLC, creating feedback loops that correct, finetune and enhance the product as it is developed.

The four quadrants of the *Analytics Product Life Cycle* (APLC) are:

- o Business
- o Data engineering
- o Modeling
- o Software engineering

The stages of the *Analytics Product Life Cycle* (APLC) encompass the following processes:

- Frame the business problem and the scope of the project
- Evaluate the organizational culture
- Identify a sponsor
- Create a team
- Collect and process data
- Build an advanced analytics model
- Validate, verify, and iterate
- Implement, test, and iterate.Embed analytics in organizational workflows and facilitate user adoption

Essential Takeaways:

- An analytics model attempts to translate a natural world phenomenon into mathematical relations by learning and extracting hidden patterns, relationships, or trends in the data. The process of assimilating real-world relationships—represented by data sets whose relationships and logic are defined by an algorithm—into a model is called *model development*.
- The model building life cycle includes data discovery, collection, processing, modeling, validation, verification, and iteration.
- Advanced analytics requires extensive modeling and incorporation of complex business logic into the algorithms that engineers write to embody a real-world system in software.
- *Analytics engineering* refers to an AI end-to-end process involving business problem framing, data preparation, model building, automation, and embedded analytics.

Prototype to Analytics Product

Operationalization is the Analytics Product Life Cycle (APLC) segment in which the advanced analytics prototype is brought into organizational, operational practice (*Fig. 52*). At the operationalization stage, the analytics model leaves the "labs" of the advanced analytics team and is placed in the hands of the operations team to be turned into a robust analytics product. This step is referred to as proof of concept (POC), prototype-to-production handoff, or machine learning operations (MLOps).

Fig. 52: Operationalization

The MLOps life cycle involves a series of stages—build, deploy and integrate, monitor, maintain—in which the model is fine-tuned, tested, updated, and enmeshed in existing organizational workflows *(Fig. 53)*. This critical last mile of the APLC involves not only the back-end prototype-to-production deployment of the analytics product by operations engineers. It is also the stage at which the results produced by the analytics model are made accessible to the organization's general user population through analytics software applications. As such, the operationalization phase should be the culmination of the APLC, the point at which the full value of the analytics product is realized. As we learned in the introduction to this book, however, 80% of analytics projects are inadequately operationalized and poorly understood in the organizations where they are introduced (Gartner, 2019).[97]

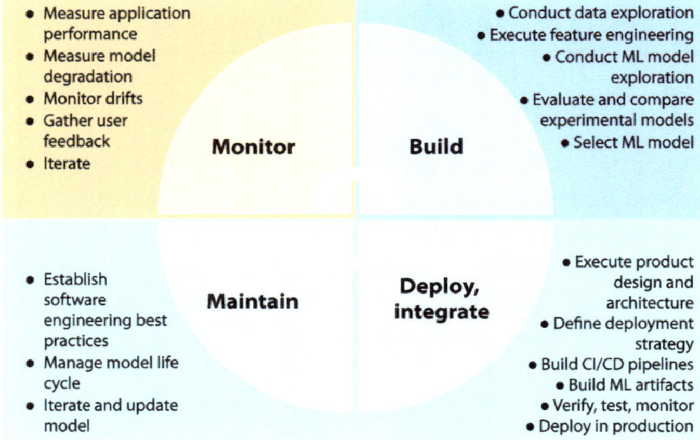

Fig. 53: Machine Learning Operations (MLOps) segments

While most organizations can derive deeper insights, uncover diverse interactions, and make rich discoveries using advanced analytics methodologies, they fall short of embedding them in workflows. *Why is this so?*

The last mile in the APLC—testing, implementation, and change management—is often ignored and seldom implemented optimally. Organizations that fail to follow through on operationalization and integrate their analytics prototypes into their workflows and processes, a step known as embedded analytics, will be unable to effect an advanced-analytics-to-AI transformation and realize the full value advanced analytics brings.

Unlike in software engineering product development, analytics products continue to evolve in an iterative process and may need continual refinement or even complete remodeling as their underlying inputs and assumptions change over time. This means that the expertise of the advanced analytics team is still needed in the MLOps phase. With analytics model development, it's never "one and done."

MLOps sits at the intersection of three disciplines: DevOps (development and operations), data engineering, and ML *(Fig. 54)*.

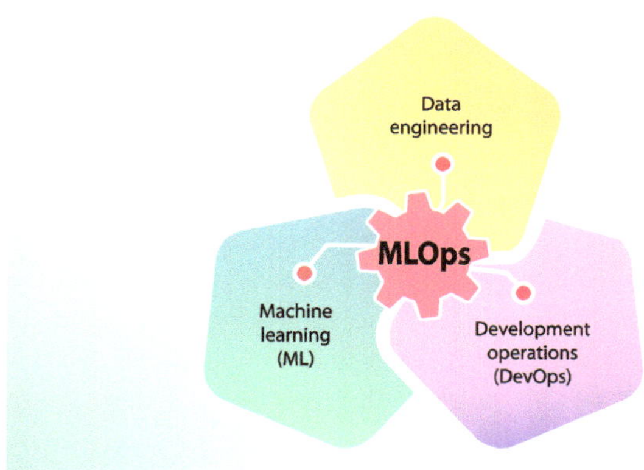

Fig. 54: Constituents of MLOps (machine learning operations)

Transferring a successful analytics prototype to a stable production environment where the analytics model is operationalized, integrated, and embedded in existing organizational business processes—and spurring user adoption of the analytics product—is not easy. An in-depth focus on change management and user adoption is vital to the success of this process but is outside the scope of this book. We will, however, cover the activity that takes place in the software engineering quadrant of the APLC and is critical to the delivery of a robust advanced analytics product.

Operationalization

Let us assume that, in our advanced analytics project, we have judiciously executed the various stages outlined in the business, data engineering, and modeling quadrants. So far, we have:

- Collected the data
- Prepared the data for modeling by performing an exploratory data analysis
- Corrected mislabeled and removed missing data (outlier detection, data cleaning)
- Normalized the features (feature processing)
- Removed extraneous features not required for modeling (feature selection)
- Created new features from the existing data (feature construction)
- Selected a machine learning model to fit to the data (model selection)
- Cherry-picked parameters that allow the most accurate model classification from the data (parameter optimization)
- Built our analytics model

Essentially, we have successfully constructed a prototype, either by developing an organic, homegrown model or by using a suite of commercially available machine learning products such as Google's Cloud AutoML, Microsoft's Azure AutoML, Amazon's SageMaker Autopilot, or an open source tool, to automate the selection, composition, and parameterization of our machine learning model. At this stage, we are ready to showcase the model's end-to-end workflow and the value that the prototype brings. We are still, however, in the research and development (R&D) phase.

Production Handoff

Handoff to the operations team commences the execution of the analytics prototype-to-production activities that comprise the software engineering quadrant. In this stage, the project is passed to operations engineers, who excel at creating repeatable, modular architecture and resilient analytics software and in deploying and maintaining data collection, transformation, analytics, and ML pipelines in operational systems (MLOps). As we have noted, this does not mean, however, that the advanced analytics team is out of the picture.

The group building the proof of concept (POC) models—the advanced analytics team—may be part of an engineering division or chief technology office (CTO) within an organization. However, the operations group responsible for deploying the model in production, maintenance, and management is often part of a centralized operational division or information technology (IT) group. The operations group is responsible for delivering the advanced analytics software. Its role is to elevate the imperfect POC model or prototype—often built with data extracts and disparate open source software that is stitched together and limited in functionality and scope—to software product delivery standards. The expertise of the advanced analytics team will be required as the model is tweaked and adapted, and the two teams should collaborate closely and effectively, ignoring organizational boundaries and hierarchies to work as one unit.

According to Algorithmia's *2020 State of Enterprise Machine Learning* report,[98] approximately 25% of a data scientist's time is spent on deployment efforts and liaising with the operations team. This time investment is required to transform the model—which, as we have mentioned, may be built on data extracts or relatively limited testing—into a ready, reliable, and secure AI analytics product.

The prototype-to-production stage is as important as the previous stages highlighted in the APLC and involves building robust software, handling model edge cases, validating the model on a periodic basis, fixing bugs, and monitoring software performance to achieve the objectives of the advanced analytics project.

Deployment of ML models in production differs from deployment of standard software engineering applications. Why is that so? As new data comes in, the input to ML models is constantly changing, impacting the accuracy of predictions or model optimizations. For this reason, models require periodic tuning, refinement, and upgrades. In extreme situations, an analytics prototype may require complete remodeling after it has been put into production. Model upgrades may be necessitated by black swan events (the COVID-19 pandemic and

---

98   https://info.algorithmia.com/hubfs/2019/Whitepapers/The-State-of-Enterprise-ML-2020/
       Algorithmia_2020_State_of_Enterprise_ML.pdf

the war in Ukraine are two recent examples). Indeed, the interdependence of the modeling and operationalization phases of the APLC is such that, in AI-mature organizations, the team building the prototype and deploying it in production is often one and the same.

Complicating the production phase is the problem of bias in the customer-facing ML models used in analytics products. Constant monitoring must occur in the model-building phase, and robust checks and balances must be in place before an analytics product is delivered. As we have discussed, an advanced analytics model is only as good as the data it is given and the business assumptions and domain knowledge that are incorporated in the algorithm-building phase, during which human bias can creep in. AI bias and ethics are essential issues to consider, although they comprise a topic that is too large, in its own right, to cover in depth in this book.

Machine Learning Operations (MLOps)

MLOps is defined as, *"a practice for collaboration and communication between data scientists and operations professionals to help manage the production ML (or deep learning) lifecycle. Similar to the DevOps or DataOps approaches, MLOps looks to increase automation and improve the quality of production ML while also focusing on business and regulatory requirements."*[99]

We will now examine the steps involved in MLOps: build, deploy, maintain, and monitor.

1. Build

Engineers building ML models may use the Python, R, Java, or Scala languages, or commercial Auto ML solutions, to create product prototypes. They pull data from various organizational and external data streams and perform a transformation to boost the performance of the models they build. Data filtering, distilling, aggregation, summarization, labeling, outlier removal, and feature engineering are some of the steps typically addressed in this process. They use diverse modeling optimization and simulation techniques, ML algorithms, and statistical models to build predictive and prescriptive models based on the business use case.

As mentioned previously, there can be a distinct difference between the models deployed in production and the models (prototypes) researched, developed, and tested in the development environment. The analytics and operations teams need to work closely together after the prototype is handed off to the operations team to ensure that the nuances of the ML model components and data pipelines are well-designed and not lost in the production environment. After the prototype-to-production handoff, however, the majority of the workload falls on the operations team, with the analytics team playing an advisory or consultative role. It is the operations team that owns the machine learning operations (MLOps) process and

---

99   https://www.bmc.com/blogs/mlops-machine-learning-ops/

that will need to ensure robust and scalable production to reduce potential risks associated with real-time, model-based decision-making.

The integration of a new analytics model into existing operational processes is painstaking work. Analytics project adoption will be impeded if the results of the model load too slowly or if the software is unreliable. User adoption is dependent upon the ability of the operations team to build high-quality, robust analytics software applications without compromising on application security, performance, or resilience. Robust and functional software applications also help to alleviate deployment pipeline friction during the change management process, when existing business needs must be balanced with technology changes.

2. Deploy, Integrate

The deployment and integration of the analytics software with existing data pipelines and operational systems involves additional considerations. Analytics software scalability and usability model and platform upgrades must also be factored in. If the goal of the analytics project is organizational process augmentation, the deployment and integration of the analytics software module into existing business applications or operational business processes must be performed with care and precision. Further, it is advisable to create REST (representational state transfer) frameworks and an API to access model artifacts and applications using containerized or microservice architecture to allow for flexible scalability and elasticity.

3. Maintain

This stage includes management of the model lifecycle after the analytics software product is deployed and integrated. Issues that must be addressed include version control testing, provenance, analytics feature testing, end-to-end analytics application testing, feature enhancements, model upgrades, model retraining and model error tracking. Beyond the software code versioning required in DevOps practice, MLOps requires the tracking of model versions, data used for model training, hyperparameters, and metadata. At this stage, critical stakeholder education should also be underway to facilitate adoption by end users, and user feedback should be sought and factored into ongoing upgrades.

The analytics and operations teams work together to optimize model improvements; iterate on existing ML models; and add new features and processes to increase operational reliability and quality of service for analytics software application users.

4. Monitor

After a model has been deployed, it must be continually monitored for prediction accuracy, simulation, optimization results, model fairness, and other important business criteria to provide complete visibility into its general business impact. These issues are monitored via BI tools (commercial or organic) connected to model outputs or through regularly scheduled reports on all critical business KPIs. Accuracy and other KPIs can be improved manually, through occasional iteration with input from a human expert, or automatically, through ongoing retraining and champion-challenger loops executed with human oversight, for example.

According to Gartner's 2021 *Magic Quadrant Report on Data Science and Machine Learning Platforms*, organizations rely heavily on open source and public cloud service provider offerings for MLOps.[100] McKinsey's *State of AI 2021* research also indicates that 64% of survey respondents rely heavily on public cloud providers for their AI workload.[101] According to McKinsey, we can attribute this trend to the widespread availability of scalable, elastic, efficient, predictable, and OPEX-friendly cloud-based options and to the myriad open source software (OSS) technology connectors that cloud technology offers. As we discussed in Chapter 6 (*Managing Data for Transformational Analytics*) OSS provides enterprises the opportunity to get up and running with little upfront cost. OSS usage is so pervasive that popular MLOps platform vendors like DataBricks, Amazon Sagemaker, and Microsoft's AutoML rely on OSS, starting with Python, the most commonly used language. DSML platform providers also help optimize and curate OSS distributions.

The process of operationalizing an analytics product can vary from organization to organization, depending upon factors such as the organization's size, resources, technological sophistication, skill sets, and risk tolerance. The type of data required for this process—real-time vs. batch processing—and the type of models used in the analytics project are key differentiators. The MLOps and analytics group may make a custom design for each project they carry out.

Visualization: Creating a Compelling Data Story

At this point in the APLC, the analytics team has identified the business questions to answer; created business problem statements; aligned on project goals; progressed through the various stages of the APLC; iterated and captured the analytics logic; and stored the results in a database. Surely it must be time to schedule the project retrospective or lessons-learned session, declare victory, and organize the end-of-project team lunch? Not so fast! Now we must turn our attention to the analytics application front-end, which is often referred to as the presentation layer or the BI or reporting dashboard.

Even if our analytics team has developed an intelligent algorithm behind the scenes that increases efficiency and revenue and reduces cost by some magical number, the project is not yet complete. From a software application development standpoint, everything that we have accomplished in the APLC—data collection, management, unified analytics platforms (UAPs), databases, analytics logic, modeling, and development—can be classified as server-side or back-end deployment. Without a presentation layer to render the resulting data

---

100 https://venturebeat.com/2021/03/14/gartners-2021-magic-quadrant-cites-glut-of-innovation-in-data-science-and-ml/

101 https://www.mckinsey.com/business-functions/mckinsey-analytics/our-insights/global-survey-the-state-of-ai-in-2021

intelligible to those who are not analytics experts, the analytics product will have very limited utility.

Advanced analytics algorithmic results are stored in a table. While the tabulated results and numbers may be meaningful at first glance to the members of the analytics team, they will likely appear incomprehensible to most users.

Close to 65% of humans are visual learners.[102] Couple this fact with the short attention spans cultivated in a digital world characterized by constant interruptions and it is easy to see why the results of an advanced analytics project can only be understood by the average person if they are translated into a presentation layer or dashboard. Dashboards are designed to tap into the brain's ability to make associations in data, perceive dimensions, and detect and differentiate color, shape, and pattern. In short, the front-end presentation layer must create story and context around raw data, facilitating instantaneous user understanding.

Succinct and straightforward are the watchwords here. The end user does not care how much data the analytics team has collected, what fancy state-of-the-art analytics technologies have been used in model building, or how hard the project teams have worked to build the analytics product that is now in operation. All of the back-end work must now be packaged into a presentation layer that provides the crucial information in an appealing interface and jumpstarts user adoption. Translating abstract statistical and mathematical information into well-conceived and well-designed intuitive graphical formats is essential. If the end-product is not accessible to users in all tiers of the organization, it will not be adopted, and the fruit of the analytics project will die on the vine.

More and more giant corporations are coming to realize the importance of an engaging user interface (UI) and a satisfying user experience (UX). Many are engaging usability design consultants in addition to front-end engineers early on in advanced analytics projects to begin the work of creating an intuitive presentation layer. Their goal is to provide attractive, elegant, intuitive, accessible dashboards that provide a clear view of organizational processes and bottlenecks, as well as the overall state of the business, as revealed by the analytics product.

A one-size-fits-all approach does not work on the application front end. Instead, dashboard displays should be appropriately tailored to user roles. An employee on the floor of an airplane assembly line who is responsible for the supply chain division may need to find out the status of a rare fuselage shipment on a cargo ship, for example. This employee may also require a detailed, drill-down view of all the pieces and components in the supply chain process. His organization head, on the other hand, may not be interested in this kind of in-the-weeds view of one narrow area of the business.

To perform their respective jobs effectively, these two different members of the organization need just the information that matters to them, and they expect this information to be

---

102   https://www.ncbi.nlm.nih.gov/pmc/articles/PMC6513874/

delivered within seconds. They don't want to wade through screens full of miscellaneous detail to locate the nugget of data they are looking for, so the information must be intuitively organized and presented in clear graphics. After all, as the adage goes, a picture is worth a thousand words.

Analytics Dashboard Categories

Picture the CEO who takes a daily pulse check of how things are functioning in her organization from an app on her phone as part of her early morning routine. A cursory glance at her corporation's *mission control* dashboard tells her everything she needs to know about her organization's KPIs, even before she gets up from bed or grabs her favorite beverage and heads to work. Just as the commercial pilot can assess whether there is enough fuel to cover a flight with just a quick glance at the cockpit dashboard's fuel gauge, the CEO uses the dashboard to obtain a quick answer to the question, *"How are we doing?"*

For the purpose of decision-making, the pilot doesn't need to know the grade of the fuel used; the number of gallons to the 10th decimal place; whether it is unleaded kerosene, naphtha-based, or biofuel; or how much it costs. These details are, on the other hand, essential information for the flight engineer.

In a nutshell, dashboards must provide an effective birds-eye view of the metrics required for each user. Role-based dashboards allow business users to extract, monitor and analyze valuable, actionable insights tailored to the appropriate level of detail for their function.

A dashboard provides a single entry point into an organization, supporting past and future data-driven decision-making. Selecting the right metrics or KPIs to display is as important as effective dashboard design.

In addition to being segmented based on user roles, dashboards can also be categorized based on the type of question or problem they are trying to address.

1. ***Operational dashboards***: These dashboards grant a comprehensive view of systems and processes within an organizational function. They offer snapshots of an organizational unit's performance and are typically monitored throughout the day. They are well suited for wall displays on a manufacturing plant floor or a global internet command and control operational center. Operational dashboards usually provide a very detailed view of processes and systems within their purview, answering the question, *"What is happening now?"*

2. ***Strategic dashboards***: These dashboards align organizational goals with corporate strategic goals. They are used to track an organization's metrics and KPIs and to monitor benchmark performance to ensure that organizational goals are met. They address questions such as the following:

   - *How did we do on metric X in this quarter compared to last quarter?*
   - *How are we doing overall?*
   - *Did our performance improve or decline in a given period?*

While operational dashboards focus heavily on specific systems, processes or business units, strategic dashboards pull data from a variety of data sources and rely on complex algorithmic logic to showcase company-wide goals and metrics.

Front-end Application Skills and Solutions

A particular set of skills is needed to build analytics dashboards. Companies hire front-end engineers with experience in HTML, CSS, React, Angular, Rest API, D3, Vue, Highcharts, or other charting technologies and programs to build their organization's *mission control* dashboards. These dashboards should conceal complex analytics logic and be simple, intuitive, enlightening, insightful, easy to use and interact with, and conducive to collaboration. Most importantly, they should be aesthetically pleasing and visually impactful, while supporting the goals and objectives of the analytics project.

In addition to hiring engineers, companies should engage user interface (UI) and user experience (UX) designers with expertise in designing user-friendly and accessible dashboards. Engaging these designers pays dividends in terms of the end-product's accessibility and usability features.

According to the World Wide Web Consortium (W3C) Web Accessibility Initiative (WAI), "Accessibility, usability, and inclusion are closely related aspects in creating a web that works for everyone."[103] Engaging UI and UX designers at the application front end is of paramount importance in creating top-quality, user-friendly dashboards that cater to all, not just a limited subset of an organization's population. For example, well-designed dashboards also make information accessible to non-visual learners, users with lower visual acuity, and those with color blindness. Creating products that work not just for a few, but for all, facilitates higher ROI.

Instead of building their own dashboards, some organizations rely on inexpensive, off-the-shelf software visualization solutions such as Tableau, Cognos, Qlick, and PowerBI, to provide intuitive, drill-down dashboards that allow users to interact with advanced analytics and artificial intelligence platforms.

Whatever solution is chosen, organic or commercial, dashboards serve the purpose of reducing or removing the technical barrier to interacting with data and data platforms. These solutions fuel accelerated data democratization and enable self-serviceability. Using specific dashboards tailored to their job function, employees can play with the data and create visualizations on their own. They can infer based on data and provide insights and recommendations to their leaders. User-friendly dashboards thus allow organizations to take small steps towards what should be their ultimate goal, reaching the *Data as a Horizontal* paradigm.

---

103   https://www.w3.org/WAI/fundamentals/accessibility-usability-inclusion/

The Downside of "Click and Viz"

As we have discussed, deconstructing, simplifying, and translating complex information into bite-size portions and formats that are comprehensible to lay users is a critical part of any organizational analytics effort. In the last decade, there has been an explosion in the range and availability of inexpensive, user-friendly, and affordable visualization tools. The availability and ease of use of "click and viz," "shake and bake," and "drag and drop" visualization options have, however, introduced one serious pitfall that can halt an organization's analytics transformation in its tracks.

Visualization tools have become so easy to use and are so appealing in their provision of instant answers that users aren't motivated to understand what lies behind the attractive graphics on their screens. The average user is not required to have any specific domain knowledge, any understanding of the sources, quality or context of the data used, or any insight into the assumptions built into the analytics models they rely on to make potentially consequential decisions. Instead, dashboards present their results as a fait accompli.

The goal of AI is to find hidden patterns in data. We live in a messy, noisy world in terms of data signal processing. Unfortunately, golden nuggets of information about the world around us are not attainable in a format that automatically lends itself to the application of AI concepts. Nor are the business problems we want to solve so perfectly aligned with AI techniques that one can directly apply them without much forethought. There is a disconnect. As we have seen throughout this book, an intermediate stage, *analytics engineering*—in which the AI concepts are tailored to business problems—bridges this divide, but the inner workings of this stage are generally opaque to anyone but those directly engaged in this process.

This opacity remains a fundamental drawback in how the discipline has evolved. Some business leaders assume that finding answers to complex business problems is as simple as point-and-click. Entry-level data scientists assume business problems will be pre-configured to fit the ML models they have learned in their academic programs.[104] It is the advanced analytics team that must balance the needs of the business, available resources, and organizational culture with technology concepts.

The reality is that visualization falls into the discipline of descriptive analytics and business intelligence (BI), requiring the rigor and scientific thinking and experimentation, verification, and validation we introduced in the earlier chapters. Users' lack of understanding of the scope, goals and logic that have gone into that deceptively simple-looking dashboard can lead to failed organizational analytics initiatives and discourage an organization from funding future analytics projects.

Consider the CEO from our earlier example, who consults her corporation's strategic dashboard to identify how various business verticals or pillars, such as finance, engineering, sales, marketing, or manufacturing, are doing with respect to organizational goals set for

---

104   https://www.techrepublic.com/article/data-science-skills-gap/

the quarter. The CEO sets up a follow-up meeting with the head of an underperforming team to find out why it missed its goals.

The leader of this underperforming team, who needs to understand and communicate why growth has slowed, turns to a dashboard for answers. The apparent simplicity of the dashboard, however, conceals complex analytics logic and other parameters with which the team leader is unfamiliar. The complex processes going on beneath the dashboard are visible to nobody outside the multidisciplinary team of business experts, engineers, and UI/UX designers who have developed the strategy and executed the data collection, processing and modeling that underpin the finished product. Unfortunately, without understanding the logic and context behind the results displayed on the dashboard, the end user—the leader of the underperforming team—cannot know for sure which questions the dashboard can and cannot answer. The team leader reports back to the CEO, quoting metrics that may well fall short of providing answers that are responsive to the actual questions at hand.

In an executive or board room setting, where time is of the essence, a poorly designed chart, flawed analytics logic, or unvalidated data will provoke tangential discussions and fruitless verbal gymnastics. They may also lead to poorly founded decisions. A well-designed dashboard created by engineers, business representatives and UX/UI designers who are aligned on business goals and D&A strategy—and well-informed users who have been trained to understand the strategy and data context beneath the dashboard's engaging graphics—will prevent this unfortunate outcome. Rigorously designed dashboards and an informed user population will promote operational excellence and create opportunities for operational innovation. This will facilitate investment and commitment to further opportunities, while minimizing risk and reducing costs.

Analytics Product Adoption

Analytics product adoption is the last mile of the prototype-to-analytics-product journey and the user representative, executive sponsor and domain expert on the analytics project team can play a vital role in encouraging user engagement with a newly operationalized analytics product, functioning as change agents. Some organizations also hire change management consultants to facilitate the analytics product adoption process, with the help of the user representative, domain expert, and executive sponsor. Listed below are a few pivotal tasks this group must perform to enable successful analytics product adoption.

- Analytics technology evolution:
  - Participating in prototype-to-production analytics software deployment ideation
  - Evaluating and monitoring results
  - Generating feedback loops to improve analytics products
  - Analyzing the impact of the analytics product on legacy processes
  - Recognizing and revealing the organization's technical, process, software, system, infrastructure, and data gaps

- o Facilitating easy software access and usability
- o Supporting organizational skill development and workload assessment and providing incentives to change behavior

- Change management:

  - o Creating analytics product awareness
  - o Bridging the technical and business gap
  - o Creating a common language around data
  - o Thoroughly assessing the impact of analytics project implementation on people, processes, and existing software
  - o Mitigating the drastic impact of new analytics products on organizational rhythm, people, processes, and software
  - o Considering alternatives if the implementation is difficult
  - o Iterating product releases and limiting organizational culture shock
  - o Providing feedback to engineers

As with any other organizational and process change, the adoption of analytics projects requires humans to change their behavior patterns. A successful push for user adoption calls for proactive leadership from influential figures who will serve as product evangelists. Enthusiastic endorsement by business leaders is especially critical if an analytics project uncovers new insights that require employees and managers to change deep-seated processes and learn new technology. The organization will need to provide support and training to facilitate employees' technological career growth.

APLC design may be quite variable within and between organizations, with the following factors playing a role:

- Size of the organization
- Type of project
- Level of technology in place
- Presence of technologically savvy leadership
- Resources available
- Risk tolerance
- Ability to innovate and evolve
- Data literacy

The prototype-to–production deployment phase is similarly fluid. The product adoption process must be recalibrated to each new analytics product, or even each feature, depending on the project's complexity, the type of models used, and the business problem being tackled.

On the technical side of this equation, testing and model validation must be performed when the code is moved from an analytics sandbox, where discovery and initial development take place, to a production environment with operational data flows. Unfortunately, this is not automatic—significant planning must be done, and the purchase, installation, and maintenance of hardware and software can be a huge undertaking for organizations with limited resources. Software best practices must be introduced to operationalize systems, data feeds and automating models. If the analytics project is a feature being added to an existing software application, additional testing and integration strategies, updated software and packages, and attention to backward compatibility must be included in the deployment process.

To Summarize:

In this chapter, we explored the handoff of the analytics prototype to the engineers responsible for the software engineering quadrant of the APLC, also known as the machine learning operations (MLOps) phase. MLOps consists of four key stages: build, deploy/integrate, maintain, and monitor. It is during this quadrant of the APLC that the analytics model becomes a product that is operationalized and embedded in organizational workflows. This critical last mile of the APLC is led by operations engineers, who work in collaboration with the advanced analytics team to ensure that the nuances of the ML model components and data pipelines are well-designed. Critically, this is also the stage during which dashboards must be created to provide an interface between the analytics model and the end-user and create a story that contextualizes the data.

Dashboards make the results of the analytics model accessible to the end user. Change management is a critical part of the rollout of a new analytics product. Organizations that fail to devote sufficient resources and attention to the operationalization of an analytics model, and to dashboards and user adoption efforts, will fall short of realizing the full value of their advanced analytics investment.

Essential Takeaways:

- Operationalization is the segment in the *Analytics Product Life Cycle* (APLC) where the analytics software prototype is brought into organizational operational practice.
- The operationalization phase of analytics product development—which includes the build, deploy/integrate, maintain, and monitor stages—is known as the ML operations life cycle (MLOps).
- In the MLOps phase, operations engineers employ diverse modeling optimization and simulation techniques, ML algorithms, and statistical models to build predictive and prescriptive models based on the business use case.
- The resulting analytics product is then deployed and integrated with existing data pipelines and operational systems.
- Throughout this quadrant of the APLC, the analytics model must be continually tested, upgraded and retrained, and monitored for prediction accuracy, simulation, optimization results, model fairness and other important factors.
- Once the back-end deployment of the analytics product has been accomplished, software applications engineers or analysts with click-viz software tools create dashboards to make it accessible to the end user.

- Fundamental questions to answer before creating a dashboard for your organization include the following:

    a. *Who is this dashboard for?*
    b. *What is the problem being addressed?*
    c. *How is this information going to be used?*

- Dashboards should be appropriately tailored to users' roles, subject matter purview, and responsibilities.
- The rollout of a new analytics product should be accompanied by rigorous change management and data literacy efforts so users gain a thorough understanding of the product's capabilities and parameters.

Chapter 9

Your Analytics Journey

There is no one universally prescribed way to do advanced analytics. Every organization that embarks upon an analytics transformation will follow its own path, determined by its size; the scope of the problems it faces; its available technology, budget, and resources; its internal culture; and the industry in which it operates.

While there is no such thing as a one-size-fits-all approach to advanced analytics, however, there are certain foundational steps and prerequisites that must be a top priority for any business wishing to harness the power of advanced analytics. These factors recur as fundamental concepts throughout this book because they are critical for organizations that want to start their analytics journey on the right foot, chart a productive course, anticipate and avoid roadblocks, and overcome unforeseen challenges.

D&A Strategy

The journey, as we have seen, begins with intent. Companies must set a purposeful D&A strategy, one that directly addresses real business challenges and is founded on well-defined problem statements that are aligned with the organization's overarching goals. For many businesses, it is beneficial to start small, focusing their early analytics efforts on a narrowly tailored business question or problem that is confined to one segment of their organization.

Organizations that take this approach can capitalize on a "fail fast and learn fast" iterative development philosophy without the risks inherent in a larger or more grandiose plan and are more likely to see their projects through to completion and implementation. When smaller-scale analytics components are embedded in organizational, operational processes and functions, surface design flaws and software bugs can be quickly identified and fixed without inordinate disruption. Measured, carefully planned rollouts of smaller-scale analytics products also help minimize the organizational culture shock that can occur in response to analytics transformation.

Even if businesses do choose to narrow their focus in this way, however, the decision to do analytics will open bigger horizons and implicate larger questions. Thus, every project, no matter how small, must fit into clearly stated organizational goals and a cohesive D&A strategy that is transparent and comprehensible to personnel at all levels.

In a relatively recent paradigm shift, some tech-savvy organizations with mature UAPs are making a lean development strategy their primary modus operandi by adopting *federated analytics*. Just as a newer school of thought has emerged to challenge centralized data architecture and the Single Source of Truth (SSOT) paradigm, leading to the development of innovations such as data mesh and data fabric, federated analytics brings decentralization to the structuring of the D&A function across business units.

In federated analytics, individual business analytics units are organized like self-governing states under a centralized analytics function. Smaller, high-performing analytics teams build prototypes to test the validity of advanced analytics algorithms. They benefit from the "fail fast and learn fast" strategy described above and can innovate rapidly. If a prototype is successful, it is promoted to a production state and a *minimum viable product (MVP)* is built and released to users. Based on user feedback, the MVP is then improved upon and refined in an iterative process. (*Fig. 55*) This approach gives individual business units greater autonomy and the independence to innovate and can offer greater agility and flexibility than a hierarchical, top-down management approach.

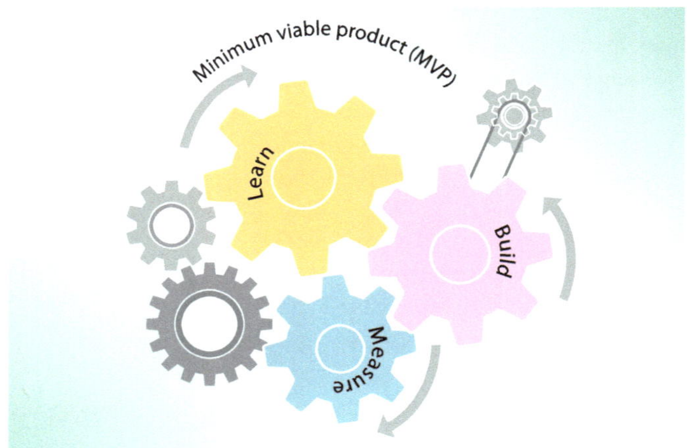

Fig. 55: Minimum viable product (MVP) – build, learn, measure feedback

Determining whether a centralized approach to analytics is right for your organization or whether a federated approach—or some other customized variant—would be more beneficial is a process that can be facilitated by an analytics consultant. Not all organizations have an infrastructure or culture that is conducive to federated analytics but, for those that do, this approach can increase profitability and revenue, reduce waste, and move them closer to reaching their organizational goals.

It is important to note that, in federated analytics, the work of decentralized analytics units must still occur under the umbrella of a unified D&A strategy that is based on a shared set of business goals. And it is critical that these goals are communicated clearly across all levels of the business. If members of an organization are entrusted with an understanding of the significance and usefulness of its analytics efforts, they will be more likely to fully support them and help see them to fruition. They will also be more likely to adopt the new analytics products that result.

If an organization fails to develop and share a thoughtful, unified D&A strategy, it won't matter how much it invests in state-of-the-art technology, the latest analytics architecture, or the most elegant software development solutions. Its projects will flounder or fail to gain traction and it will stall in its analytics journey.

Analytics Fitness

As we have seen throughout this book, analytics transformation can be achieved only with sufficient investment in infrastructure, people, software, and technology—including the all-important development of a unified analytics platform to store and rationalize all organizational data in a manner that aligns with business context.

Businesses that wish to implement advanced analytics must hire talented engineers with experience in advanced analytics, cloud computing, and Big Data technologies. They must also ensure that they have a robust data ecosystem that can seamlessly support every step of the data life cycle. This ecosystem must be equipped with the infrastructure to support ML frameworks, statistical packages and programming languages, connectors to structured and unstructured data, cloud services, and data collection services that collect, store, and analyze data for both operational and research/strategic advanced analytics workloads. With the growth of cloud and Big Data platforms, technologies that can take organizations from data collection to advanced analytics products are becoming increasingly plentiful and affordable, bringing analytics within reach for organizations of all sizes.

Reaching and maintaining peak Analytics Fitness is feasible, however, only if companies take the golden nuggets of knowledge generated by advanced analytics prototypes and operationalize and build them into analytics products that they then embed in existing workflows and processes, with pre-defined, auditable, repeatable, automated steps. Implementing automation and embedded analytics is a vital step for organizations that want to realize the economic value and measurable benefits of their analytics efforts, but it is also a complicated and potentially expensive process that requires expert knowledge, negotiation between business and analytics teams, and careful finessing during rollout.

On the technical side, embedding analytics in existing processes will require upfront expenditure. In this critical last mile of the Analytics Product Life Cycle, team business and team analytics must not lose sight of the ultimate objectives of the analytics project at hand and must have a shared understanding of the challenges associated with reaching these objectives. To save costs and facilitate an easier functional integration of analytics insights into existing processes, team business may be willing to live with a model that offers 80% accuracy, instead of holding out for a model that offers 95% accuracy but may be harder to deploy and integrate into operational business processes. At this juncture, team analytics and team business should consider tradeoffs, negotiate, and come to an agreement that both sides can tolerate.

At the rollout stage, the benefits of a robust and clearly articulated D&A strategy come into play. Here, the foundational work of aligning D&A strategy with meaningful business goals and sharing those goals across the organization will help to bring about a shift in organizational culture. Having influential, visionary leaders in the upper echelons of management and skilled senior engineers and architects with tribal knowledge of the organization will be indispensable in helping to achieve stakeholder alignment and ensuring that the project has the necessary technical support.

Change management and training initiatives will also be vital in overcoming organizational inertia. Knowledge workers may be unwilling to give up control or trust automation because of the fear of the unknown or because of mainstream organizational barriers that restrict the free movement of ideas, and people. Upskilling these employees, providing information-sharing forums, and investing in intangible areas such as data governance, self-serviceability, and data literacy will go a long way toward overcoming this resistance. Employees who see the value of automation and who are cognizant of the big picture will not only be primed for success but will also help smooth the way for the widespread adoption of embedded analytics technology.

If analytics projects are done right, one successful project will lead to more projects, as prior art, data foundations, and insights mined from each successfully completed project will engender a jumping off point for the next.[105] As data projects spread, the number of users will increase, and more data sources will be formally managed. More users will see the merit of using automated data platforms for reporting instead of error-prone, manual spreadsheets. Users involved in projects requiring significant human-centric interaction and involvement to access non-scalable legacy data systems will clamor for better applications and automated analytics workflows. Managers invited to repetitive, time-consuming meetings to outline logic in the era of zoom fatigue and remote work will insist on better decision-making tools.

As organizational processes and underlying technologies become more complex, both internal and external users will demand further investment in analytics decision-making platforms and streamlined procedures. And, as analytics competence becomes common currency, individual business units will be better equipped to handle their own analytics functions and accelerate innovation in alignment with organizational goals and objectives.

Advanced analytics will upend old, laborious, non-auditable business practices and simplify processes by providing humans in-the-loop applications that revamp operational efficiencies. These changes will build on one another to accelerate analytics transformations and move organizations to the highest levels of Analytics Fitness.

Data as a Horizontal

The decision to adopt advanced analytics is an inherently transformational one. As described above, even modest analytics projects shed light on inefficiencies in business practices and open the door to new insights and ways of thinking. The more expansive the reach of analytics in an organization—and the higher its level of Analytics Fitness—the

---

105   https://online.hbs.edu/Documents/a-beginners-guide-to-data-and-analytics.pdf?hsCtaTracking=2bb079d4-
       1f8a-4052-9548-2430ccb52d48%7C4d888017-3b60-48fb-abd2-754f4106abb4

more visibility there will be into its business and operational processes, enabling creative and forward-thinking solutions to previously intractable challenges.

When implemented successfully, embedded analytics can be an intrinsically democratizing force. Its fundamental impetus is to foster a culture of knowledge propagation and transparency by expanding access to data and understanding. In organizations that are truly data-driven, analytics will not be limited to restricted sets of people cloistered in high-performing functional groups. Instead, data access will spread horizontally, energizing employees in all tiers of the organization to use analytics in their day-to-day work, taking ownership of objectives and doing their part to help the organization reach them.

Managers and aspiring managers in such organizations may become power users of advanced analytics technologies, transforming themselves into citizen analysts and citizen ML users. They, in turn, will help to perpetuate the further spread of Data as a Horizontal, imbuing workers at all levels with a sense of ownership and shared responsibility previously limited to the upper echelons of leadership.

While some forward-looking executives will welcome this transformation with open arms, leaders in legacy organizations with siloed domains and entrenched power structures may be less likely to embrace the transparency and democratizing cultural ramifications of transformational analytics. Where competition and insecurity reign, whether due to the tone set by leadership or the effects of longstanding dysfunction in an organization's internal culture, reactions to the changes wrought by analytics can range from suspicion to outright hostility (*Fig. 56*).

Fig. 56: Dysfunctional analytics team

Some executives, unsettled by the light that analytics sheds on business inefficiencies in their units, may be motivated by the unwelcome, inconvenient nature of these insights to undercut analytics and the value it brings. Other leaders may feel the need to protect, claim, influence, and own coveted D&A projects in the hope of being perceived as thought leaders in their organizations. Instead of taking a collaborative approach, they may generate ongoing turf wars over which team should "own" D&A. Discussions may revolve around highly charged terms like "I," "mine," and "yours," and a preoccupation with hierarchy and titles may pit leadership and the rank and file against one another. In such organizations, siloed groups that commandeer analytics technology may even use it as a means of defeating management direction.

These issues highlight the importance of having technology-savvy management capable of forging clear organizational goals, charting a meaningful D&A strategy, achieving buy-in and alignment across multidisciplinary teams, and keeping everyone marching in the same direction. When analytics is undermined from within organizational fiefdoms or a company's technology and its application is hijacked by a particular group, that is not a failure of analytics; it is a failure of management.

When initiating organizational analytics transformation projects, management should therefore ensure that organizational culture is factored into its D&A strategy. As we have discussed, fostering collaboration and communication, upskilling employees, and offering easy-to-use unified analytics platforms with intuitive user interfaces are foundational steps that lay the groundwork for successful data democratization. This combination of collaboration, data literacy and data access will be mutually reinforcing, helping to propel organizations ever higher on their Analytics Fitness journey, toward Data as a Horizontal.

Becoming Data-Driven

Becoming a data-driven organization is a journey that unfolds over time. As the cliché goes, "It's a marathon, not a sprint." Progress toward Analytics Fitness and a horizontal data culture is typically measured in years, and sometimes decades, especially in non-technology-focused companies. There will inevitably be challenges and setbacks along the way, and not every analytics project will bear fruit. Organizations that build the necessary foundation for analytics success and commit to the journey, however, will find that analytics will enable them to unearth hidden knowledge, extract precious information, exert better control over their businesses, and even predict future challenges and opportunities.

A study published by Accenture in 2022 following a survey of more than a thousand executives from more than a thousand global firms revealed that, to date, only 12% of firms are "AI Achievers" and have reached the necessary level of AI maturity to achieve superior growth and business transformation.[106] Accenture's machine learning models suggest, however, that the number of AI Achievers is set to increase rapidly, more than doubling to 27% of companies by 2024. The study notes that the current crop of AI Achievers is reaping

---

106   https://www.accenture.com/us-en/insights/artificial-intelligence/ai-maturity-and-transformation

the rewards of innovation and that even in the pre-pandemic era they enjoyed 50% greater revenue growth than their peers.

According to 2022 data published by management consulting firm KPMG, artificial intelligence and automation stand out as particularly well established in terms of both adoption and results, while applications and regulations are still evolving and have a long way to go. Half of respondent organizations have deployed and seen positive ROI from machine learning [107]

The frequency of such reports from leading consulting firms indicates that AI investments will continue to fuel revenue growth. Major technology behemoths such as Google, Facebook, and Microsoft are already investing in the scalability of AI in diverse business sectors, with transformational results in terms of innovation and resiliency in the face of black swan events.

Business leaders who have embarked on analytics projects in their organizations are learning from their successes and becoming ever more educated about what AI can do for them. These leaders are increasingly willing to pursue proofs of concept whose business value is initially unclear and are more comfortable with taking the driver's seat on AI adoption.

In the next ten years, as the technology expands in scope and becomes increasingly cost-effective, there will not be any major vertical left untouched by AI. With rapid learning and adoption, AI has already become an undeniable part of society and something that people routinely interact with in nearly every sphere of life. It has become central to user experience and now mediates the way consumers interact with brands and technologies. Organizations that are attuned to this transformation and ready for its inexorable expansion are the ones that will thrive in the future.

The next decade will belong to those who understand the importance of data, algorithms, and computational architectures and can use the transformations in these spaces in truly effective ways. AI will continue to build on its potential to detect life-threatening diseases in the nascent stage, predict weather conditions, and find myriad other ways to grow its role as humanity's digital collaborator.

In recent years, the pace of change in the sector has been unprecedented, and it promises to continue in the same vein in the years to come. A variety of new use cases will emerge from the rapidly evolving nature of AI, which is already achieving faster computation, higher accuracy and lower computation and infrastructure costs. Organizations that create a D&A roadmap, build a UAP, and work their way up the Analytics Fitness ladder will be well positioned to enjoy increased revenue, more satisfied customers, best-in-class operating efficiencies, and improved profitability. They will also move inexorably toward achieving the Data as a Horizontal paradigm.

---

107   https://info.kpmg.us/news-perspectives/technology-innovation/kpmg-2022-technology-survey.html

Successful data-driven organizations of the future will share a common set of precepts. They will:[108,109,110]

- Establish the culture, functions, processes, and authorities necessary to control and manage enterprise data (internal and external).
- Focus on good data governance, metadata management, and data veracity.
- Collate operational and strategic data in order to make key business decisions.
- Have frameworks and metrics in place to quantify and measure the tangible and intangible value generated by data and analytics projects.
- View data as an organizational asset, not as the property of the individual departments that created or collected the data.
- Empower employees by reducing the voice gap:

  - Ensure that everyone plays a role in moving the organization forward by identifying efficiencies and opportunities that include data.
  - Provide a voice for knowledge workers in critical business decisions that will shape their future.
  - Give knowledge workers and advanced analytics practitioners a say on topics related to data and analytics digital transformation and innovative process improvement.
  - Create an environment in which workers are not penalized for identifying data and analytics-related process gaps and critical flaws in business decisions.

- Reorganize teams around data and analytics: bring businesspeople, engineers and advanced analytics practitioners together to plan and execute a cohesive D&A strategy.
- Embed data and analytics inside every business unit, while maintaining a degree of centralization.
- Promote knowledge-sharing and collaboration between business leaders, end-users, and advanced analytics practitioners to keep the data and analytics iteration process alive.
- Carefully select employees with strong technical skills and a collaborative ethic.
- Maintain a competitive advantage by continuously investing in technology, training, and development to adapt rapidly to the ever-changing data and analytics marketplace.

---

108 https://sloanreview.mit.edu/article/leading-with-decision-driven-data-analytics/

109 https://mitsloan.mit.edu/ideas-made-to-matter/5-traits-workforce-future?utm_source=mitsloan linkedin&utm_medium=social&utm_campaign=workertraits

110 https://www.accenture.com/_acnmedia/pdf-108/accenture-closing-data-value-gap-fixed.pdf

Appendix: Miners' Tales

The following is a compilation of insights from D&A practitioners with extensive experience in the manufacturing, pharmaceutical, HealthTech, and insurance sectors. Each contributor discusses an aspect of data analytics and its impact in the business environment.

Data Literacy

By Stephen Gatchell

Data literacy is vital to ensuring that companies are aligned on the mission, vision, and value of their data strategy. If data literacy is of low maturity in your company, every conversation will be a sales pitch and a challenge to get buy-in for vital resources or execution across key initiatives. Most importantly, low levels of data literacy diminish the value derived from data! Organizations with greater maturity around data literacy initiate the highest-value conversations, solve problems, and identify opportunities for data to drive impact and bring value to the company.

Data literacy tends to become more of a focus as companies mature their data strategy and execution, but, in my view, this correlation represents a backward approach. Instead, data literacy should be cultivated up-front so that it can support the development of a data strategy that aligns with an organization's corporate strategy. From the outset, as budgets, resources and timelines are planned for the execution of a data strategy, data literacy must be included as a budget line item. Data literacy resources should be identified and senior leadership should carve out time for themselves, as well as for those in their organizations, to develop mature data literacy skills. Companies that do so will reap many benefits, including attracting and retaining talent, improving customer experience, increasing operational efficiencies, and adding to their profitability.

Here are five simple questions to consider when beginning your organization's data literacy journey:

Why is there so much focus on data?

If you watched the news during the COVID-19 pandemic, you couldn't help but see a profusion of data being used in stories focused on the stock market, unemployment, and COVID-19 itself. The enormous amount of data being generated about the virus and its public health impact included the number of new cases, people recovered, and rates of partial and full vaccination, data that could then be analyzed to develop insights, formulate ideas, confirm theories or, in some cases, uncover information that was not previously known. Public officials could analyze the percentage of people vaccinated in a state like Massachusetts and compare it to other states to understand if Massachusetts was doing a good job managing the virus or needed to take stricter measures. If Massachusetts was one of the bottom five states in terms of virus prevention, the governor could decide to take additional action to increase the rate of vaccination (take action to impact the outcome). By reviewing the data to understand emerging challenges, the governor could change course and take measures like opening more vaccination centers, providing transportation to those centers, or motivating people to get vaccines by offering rewards. Data provided the means to formulate an effective response.

Why does a company need data as part of its strategy?

Companies use data across many different functions to drive analysis and insights so they can measure and determine areas of their business that are performing well and those that need focus to drive improvement. Continuing to use the COVID-19 example, during the pandemic, companies could collect external or third-party data to help direct pandemic policies across company offices. For example, data on COVID-19 infection rates tracked by government agencies across the world could help drive their own company policies. Management teams could make decisions on closing offices, allow people back into the office, set the maximum number of people in an office, and other major decisions. Taking data, analyzing its trends, and developing insights ultimately drove decisions that would keep many employees remote, impacting how people worked and ensuring they stayed healthy. Internal data was also used to understand roles and functions within companies, to determine which personnel would be required to continue in-office.

What types of data challenges can companies have?

Companies collect massive amounts of data from products, applications, operational systems, employees, customers, partners, and various external sources. Challenges include ensuring that the data they collect is of practical value (What are the right business problems to solve using data and insights?), that they have ownership over the data, and that their data collection practices are in compliance with both internal policies and external regulations. They must also ensure that the data is high-quality and fit for purpose, and that they are able to use the data to support or drive decisions. Data needs to be collected purposefully and made available to the right people, at the right time, at the right level of quality.

How can companies overcome data challenges?

First, a company must have a data strategy that is simple to understand. The data strategy must include an operating model, roles and responsibilities, goals, an intake process focused on a well-defined set of priorities, and a definition of what a "good" outcome looks like (driving data to impact and measuring that impact). There are many stakeholders who need to manage data, maintain standards, develop core processes, define skills and job categories to support end-end data strategy, and execute the operating model. Operating models can be centralized, (with all data-related activities, including data engineering, and data governance managed by a central group), decentralized (with each function operating independently) or hybrid (in which a center of excellence is established to provide standards, tools, and guardrails, with functional execution occurring where appropriate). A clear data strategy and an effective operating model should be complemented by stakeholder education around privacy and security policies and the guidance of subject matter experts.

Where should a company start to focus on data?

It is useful to begin by gaining an understanding of how data can help answer questions or solve problems. Key stakeholders should be asked about the challenges they are trying to address, the questions they are trying to answer, or the hypotheses they are trying to either prove or disprove. Once a collection of business challenges is identified, these challenges should be assessed in light of overall corporate strategy to help to prioritize which ones should be addressed first. An evaluation of data should be completed. The company should determine whether the right tools are in place to collect new data (if required), develop the visualizations needed, and create the necessary models. Stakeholders, data owners and subject matter experts should be enlisted to help drive the project to its conclusion.

Increasing data literacy across an organization can help overcome challenges throughout the analytics life cycle. While an entire book could be written about data literacy, the following are five common questions that can come up at the start of an organization's data literacy evolution:

1. *Intuition and gut feelings have been successful in the past, so why must data and insights drive decisions?*

   In organizations, and in the world at large, nothing remains static. Organizations can only grow and thrive if they are flexible enough to adapt to both internal changes and the changing conditions in which they operate. If a business has changed but decisions are still being based on past experiences and practices, the organization will not function optimally. Impacts such as COVID-19, for example, changed how consumers purchased products, shifting the point of purchase from in-store to e-commerce. Accordingly, businesses needed to adjust to a new reality. Data was crucial in identifying and validating the extent to which customer behavior had changed so that informed business decisions could be made about the critical steps that needed to be taken to meet the new demand. Past circumstances could be compared to the new reality and validated by data. Companies with high levels of data literacy were more willing to challenge past wisdom and more agile in their adaptation to new market conditions.

2. *The data and reporting we currently use is the same data and reporting we have always used. Why must we change?*

   Are the existing data and reporting driving the right outcomes today and for the future? How has the business changed? Are legacy data and reporting practices capable of capturing the present reality and forecasting future trends? Analyses of pre- vs. post-COVID consumer behavior, for example, yield very different insights. Past data can drive incorrect decisions.

3. *The data generated for a specific function is not valuable to other functions, as it is specialized information. Won't combining data across functions increase complexity without adding value?*

   How can transparency, collaboration, and thinking differently help specific business functions and the company as a whole drive better outcomes? Different types of cross-functional data can provide different perspectives on problems, identify key data needed to enhance insights, and generate diverse ideas. Continuing with our COVID-19 example, before the pandemic, companies may have conducted separate analyses of direct store sales and e-commerce sales. Maintaining that separation under the conditions generated by the pandemic would result in each business unit (in-store vs. e-commerce) gaining an incomplete picture of the new reality, making it harder for them to produce correct revenue predictions. Combining in-store and e-commerce sales, as well as other key data sets, in a single analysis would produce much greater insight into the consumer profile for the entire company.

4. *Analytics projects yield too much information and I don't have time to focus on it all. Much of the data is not relevant to me, so why should I bother with it?*

   Analytics and data literacy efforts must, above all, be relevant to their audience. Individuals trying to perform functional roles within an organization should not have to sift through an undifferentiated mass of data every time they need a data point or an answer to a question. Therefore, data must be filtered and targeted so that users are not required to navigate through a torrent of extraneous results to find the nuggets of information that they need. Data literacy efforts should likewise focus on teaching end users how to find and interpret the specific data that is relevant to them. Executives need data that is broader and less granular than the information needed by workers situated within a particular business segment or function. Business leaders require results that provide holistic insight into the state of their organization in order to make data-driven decisions. As stakeholders get closer to the data, they require an education process that is more focused and specific to individual business functions. Not everyone has to be a deep subject matter expert but providing data literacy programs tailored to different organizational roles will help drive continuous learning across the organization.

5. *The data and insights we have are not good enough and we need more information and clarity before making any decisions. At what point is data actionable?*

   A balance must be reached that ensures sufficient trust in the data to inspire confidence but there should also be a cutoff point at which the data and the insights it generates are deemed fit for purpose. In data analytics, the perfect can be the enemy of the good. An important part of data literacy is understanding what is good enough. Financials must be perfect, but end-user data, engineering data, or even research data only needs to be fit for purpose in order to drive decisions.

Communicating why data and data literacy is vital to your company will take time and effort. Context and messaging must be aligned so that stakeholders at varying levels of data literacy grasp the importance and utility of the information they are given. Change management is vital. Messaging and materials must be created to drive home key points and time must be spent educating influencers across your company who can help drive the messaging. When it comes to data literacy, there are no shortcuts. It does not work when executives back an initiative in a meeting but don't really understand the commitment they are making to increasing data literacy maturity across the company. Employees in a variety of roles must have time to learn and space must be given for debate so that standard ways of doing things can be challenged and organizational changes made. A data vocabulary must be developed to drive new understanding and change mindsets so that data can be used in a meaningful and impactful way.

Data literacy is not a project or even a program. It is a foundational mindset that must be embedded in the culture of the company. If you want your corporate and data strategies to be successful, make sure you incorporate data literacy into those strategies.

Analytics and Patient Engagement in Pharma
By Brahma Tangella

The pharmaceutical industry and the healthcare community were in the spotlight during the COVID-19 pandemic, under pressure to deliver as the world faced an unprecedented health crisis. There was a significant push to leverage digital technology and other advancements to reach out to citizens during this unprecedented time. The pandemic was the ultimate forcing function, pushing organizations to speed up their digital transformation agendas across nearly all aspects of their business. Pharmaceutical companies were motivated to improve their potential peak EBITDA (earnings before interest, taxes, depreciation, and amortization) impact by leveraging data analytics, artificial intelligence, wearables, IoT, quantum computing, and other digital technologies at scale to boost output. Opportunities proliferated across research and early development, regulatory, safety, manufacturing, supply chain, and other enabling functions.

In the pharma sector, opportunities to improve patient engagement—the holy grail of healthcare—multiplied. Patient engagement involves providers and patients working together to improve health outcomes. Patients who are engaged as decision-makers in their care tend to be healthier and experience better outcomes than their counterparts who are less engaged.

Patient engagement is also key to improved patient adherence to medication schedules—a prerequisite for achieving better outcomes, fewer ER visits, fewer hospitalizations, and more satisfied patients. Failure to adhere to prescribed medication regimens is one of the principal reasons patients don't achieve the expected outcomes from their treatment. Solving this challenge has been a major goal for pharmaceutical and healthcare organizations for decades. Studies show that 50 to 60 percent of patients with chronic illnesses miss doses, take the wrong doses, and/or drop off treatment in the first year.[111]

As adherence increases, downstream medical costs decrease, as do adverse outcomes. An estimated 125,000 lives are lost annually in the United States due to noncompliance with prescription regimens, and additional healthcare expenditures of $290 billion are driven by nonadherence.[112] Solving for adherence is a win-win for everyone, especially the patient. But adherence is a complex issue that is influenced by several factors, including side effects, medication cost, dosing frequency, and routes of administration, as well as patient beliefs, demographics, and comorbidities.

While no single intervention strategy can improve the adherence of all patients, decades of research studies agree that unsuccessful patient adherence is driven by a set of key factors. These include poor patient understanding of their illness and of the prescribed medication; lack of understanding of instructions for dosage and administration of the medication; and low competence in self-management. Clear, transparent, and effective communication between health professionals and their patients leads to the growth of trust in the therapeutic relationship and can help with the challenge of patient adherence.

Today, patients have unprecedented access to their data and are amenable to sharing that data in a safe and secure manner if it will be used to improve their health outcomes. With heterogeneous sources of healthcare data becoming available from clinical, financial, and operational sources, as well as from IoT devices, wearables such as fitness trackers, self-reported tracking apps, and smart containers/medication dispensing devices, it is possible to develop a 360-degree view of a patient, in collaboration with other industry constituents. The new generation of smart, patient-friendly devices is creating a tsunami of data and a wave of new opportunities to provide intelligence analytics that lower costs and improve care outcomes. The recent emergence of wearable technologies enables the continuous monitoring of human physical activities and behaviors, as well as physiological and biochemical parameters during daily life. The wide usage of medical wearables, prompted by their affordability and convenience, has been identified as a critical development in the remote monitoring of the health of patients who accept data agreements.

The latest advances mean that these devices are now capable of collecting highly accurate patient health data and connecting remotely to the personal physician

---

111   Hayden B. Bosworth et al., "Medication adherence: A call for action," American Heart Journal, 2011, Volume 162, Issue 4, pp. 412-24, ncbi.nlm.nih.gov

112   Estimate on lives saved is from Accelerating progress in promoting prescription medicine adherence: The adherence action agenda, National Council on Patient Information and Education, October 2013, bemedwise.org; and expenditures saved is from Thinking outside the pillbox: A system-wide approach to improving patient medication adherence for chronic disease, New England Healthcare Institute (NEHI), August 2009, nehi.net.

who will then be able to monitor a patient's health progress and check if the patient is correctly using their medications. The devices themselves have the capability to analyze data over time and support patient management and disease management. The overall access component of the information flow from various data sets and various healthcare IT systems needs to be enabled by governance. The traditional approach of reactive patient care is evolving into a predictive, data-driven approach enabled by digital ecosystem apps.

Technological advances need to be combined with a patient-centric engagement model. To do this, the emphasis must shift from product-centered to patient-centered, digitally enabled solutions—all focused on delivering life-changing patient outcomes. Indeed, patient expectations and demands are creating critical challenges as well as opportunities for healthcare and pharmaceutical organizations. After all, patients are consumers in their daily lives and their expectations have been revolutionized by services offered by large technology and B2C companies like Amazon, Google, Microsoft, Walmart, eBay, and several others. To successfully ride this wave of change, pharma industry constituents need to continuously evaluate how digital disruption is changing patient behavior, rethink their patient engagement model to leverage disruptive technologies, and redesign employees' roles to maximize value for patients and enable an enhanced experience for them. Patients are increasingly seeking better service and integrated solutions and are themselves becoming catalysts for change.

The availability of high volumes of data, predictive analytics and sophisticated decision models is presenting many opportunities to improve patient adherence. The continued explosion of data will only make these algorithms better in the future. Predictive analytics can be used in a variety of ways to help identify medication nonadherent risk factors in patients. Tools that pair existing data with predictive algorithms can:

- Identify characteristics of a nonadherent population and determine which patients need timely interventions.
- Predict the potential future nonadherence of patients who are currently adherent.
- Match nonadherent patients with the best form of intervention for them (personalized decision-making) supported by digital technology.
- Close the loop and predict responsiveness and future adherence after an intervention.

Data and predictive analytics shouldn't be viewed as a panacea that will singlehandedly improve patient adherence. Instead, data and analytics solutions can provide strong early warning signals that help the critical players—pharma organizations, healthcare providers and payers in the ecosystem—assume a proactive role in preventing and correcting nonadherence. The emergence of digital tools and virtual engagement have placed the patient at the center of the universe, but every supporting organization must gear its personalized patient-centricity efforts to transform the patient experience.

These are complex problems that require intuitive, scalable solutions that allow patients to be educated, valued, heard, seen, and supported. The rapidly evolving technology landscape and the ability to leverage mobile technology, chatbots, sensors and fitness trackers to track, educate, support, and change patient behaviors on a regular basis provides a significant impetus. But to truly realize the value of patient engagement, all the critical industry constituents—pharma and medical technology organizations, healthcare providers, and payers in the ecosystem—will need to rise to the challenge and follow through at the appropriate intervention points to improve patient outcomes.

The Emerging Role of Predictive Analytics in Insurance

By Srinivasan Sankar

Predictive analytics is changing business process management in the insurance industry by providing tools and expertise to capture and analyze data, both structured and unstructured. Analytics is used in the insurance industry to predict risks. Often a score is generated that can be easily interpreted by a human or managed through an automated process. These scores are used to assess policy applicant risk, derive customer profitability, indicate claim severity, or shed light on other areas where an insurer wants to know the unknown. Predictive models do not typically feed directly into a rate decision, though a score might influence a risk tier, indirectly adjusting the rate. Listed below are the key predictive analytics use cases in the insurance industry:

- **Underwriting risk score:** Generates a single score to help underwriters (focused on evaluating the risks involved in insuring people and assets) assess potential risk.[113]
- **Profitability:** Determined by the customer's book of business and channels.
- **Customer profitability:** Aids insurers in deciding which customers are financially worth pursuing and insuring.
- **Propensity to buy:** Identifies targets for marketing a product by demographic
- factors.
- **Propensity to renew/non-renew:** Generates scores that predict current customers' likelihood of renewal.
- **Cross-sell/upsell:** Predicts opportunities to market other lines of business or higher-value options.
- **Claims severity:** Generates scores to help adjusters predict the probable severity of a claim.
- **Claims fraud:** Predicts the likelihood of fraudulent claim scores.
- **Agent/broker performance models:** Assesses new business from the perspective of past business.
- **Recovery scores:** Identify salvage and subrogation opportunities that may otherwise be missed.

---

113   https://www.investopedia.com/terms/i/insurance-underwriter.asp

Key Analytics Trends

Trends currently shaping the insurance landscape are outlined below.

Dynamic Pricing and Risk Selection

With the variety and sophistication of data sources consistently growing, information collected by insurers will be more actionable. These data sources include social media, smart devices, and interactions between claims specialists and customers. Increased modeling speed powered by ML allows insurers to explore alternative pricing strategies and unique market segments and automate product and service features instantly.

Loss Predictions for Claims, Pricing, and Reserving

Predictive analytics implements "bottom-up" loss reserving by projecting loss development for each claim and establishing an organization's estimates based on an aggregation of these individual claims. By deducing a final loss amount, the ML algorithm readily identifies the claims needing priority handling and the clusters of similar claims for corrective product/pricing action.

Claims Outliers and Transformation

Predictive analytics helps identify claims that unexpectedly become high-cost losses, known as outlier claims. Property and casualty (P&C) insurers can review previous claims for similarities and send alerts to claims specialists with proper analytics tools. A prior view of potential losses can help insurers minimize these outlier claims. Advancements in AI & other analytical tools have become increasingly important in the claims process, transforming how carriers do business.

Automated Underwriting and Portfolio Optimization

Predictive models classify current and potential risks from the lowest to highest likely loss ratios. This enables the companies to develop underwriting, pricing, and loss control strategies that correspond to the magnitude and complexity of individual risks, thus improving overall performance. Insurance underwriting models group claims by similarities. By tracking variations and changes in claim frequency, severity and time needed to close, these models can segment claims by types of loss and analyze their impact on an organization's business.

Entering Untapped Markets

Predictive analytics can help insurers identify and target potential markets. Data can reveal behavioral patterns and common demographics/characteristics so they know where to focus. With 3.2 billion people on social media, these platforms provide information crucial to the identification of potential markets. Social media has also influenced customer service: about 60% of Americans say that social media has improved their customer experience.

Customer 360-Degree View

Using predictive analytics, insurers can quickly and accurately consolidate data and generate new insights, getting a complete picture of a customer. What are their buying habits? What is their risk profile? How apt are they to buy new or expanded coverage? With modern data management solutions, predictive analytics tools can build a robust customer profile, provide cross-sell/upsell opportunities, or even forecast potential customer profitability. Using data driven insights, insurers can deliver on-demand services to their customers via the cloud with insurance data models. Before predictive analytics, insurers could only take guesses at these questions, but now they can accurately and effectively service customers, leading to happier customers and increased revenues.

With AI projects delivering extraordinary returns, producing transparent models for maintaining profitable underwriting, pricing, and claims operations is going to be required in the future and predictive analytics usage in the insurance industry is going to continue to increase.

Beware the Policy Vacuum: Healthcare Analytics

By Amanda Lord, Raymond Jorgensen, Colin Barry

Every year, provider organizations eagerly await "report cards" from Medicare that convey whether healthcare providers receive positive or negative payment adjustments from their participation in one of the Quality Payment Programs (QPP) offered by the Centers for Medicare and Medicaid Services (CMS). These programs are a part of the evolution of government-sponsored analytic initiatives rich with lessons learned. This chapter will unpack the current state of these programs from the perspective of one healthcare software vendor and Qualified Registry, Patient360, and will explore lessons learned and factors to consider in creating and managing meaningful data analytics for stakeholders.

Healthcare analytics is a large domain with many possible areas of focus. Consider how goals might differ or even compete depending upon whether one is focused on maximizing revenue vs. improving clinical outcomes for patients. This writing will focus primarily on quality, which imposes interesting data challenges. Clinicians use electronic medical/health records (EMR/EHR) systems to manage patients and workload. From ordering diagnostics to e-prescribing to capturing detail regarding an encounter, healthcare providers must meet the demands of these systems while doing their best to make patients feel heard and cared for. It may be clear to some that this process and the tools used are not yet mature. Further (and less known or understood), doctors who collaborate with one another often use completely different systems to input data for patient records, and these systems do not share data nor interact easily. Therefore, under current circumstances, using healthcare analytics on behalf of a patient inevitably involves multiple doctors and multiple disparate and competing systems.

Transparently, the authors are principals at Patient360 (www.Patient360.com). Patient360 is a Medicare-qualified registry paid by healthcare providers to collect, aggregate, score, and submit data to Medicare that benchmarks clinical performance and cost. Capturing data for this purpose is challenging as it must be collected from thousands of disparate EMR/

EHR systems, and even sometimes from paper charts. Data capture is further complicated by inconsistencies around the definition of data elements and the source and destination of those elements, and lack of clarity regarding outcomes. The latter factor is exceedingly challenging, since providers want to perform well, and registries wish to assist them. Adding yet another challenging layer, Medicare's quality payment program requires compliance with thousands of pages of rules and policies that can seem overwhelming and punitive. Most Medicare providers are obligated to participate and perform well or lose up to 9% of their fees-for-service income.

The existence and operation of Patient360 is dependent on an outside entity, CMS, which formulates and controls all policies and procedures related to the quality payment program. Like most federal agencies, CMS uses independent contractors to manage various portions of Medicare processes. For claim adjudication alone, CMS engages seven Medicare Administrative Contractors. These contractors are charged with adjudicating claims based on federal Medicare payment policy, yet they often seem to make inconsistent benefit determinations.

There are dozens of examples of the friction between CMS policy and its execution. A memorable and frustrating example occurred when CMS launched a long-awaited application programming interface for data submission. The update was intended to mitigate the manual uploading of JavaScript Object Notation (JSON) files into CMS's archaic system. This greatly anticipated update was fraught with issues. It is important to understand that CMS, like all government entities, is bound by federal policies that derive from laws created by Congress. The CMS final rule is an annual summary document resulting from months of lobbying, stakeholder inquiry, and CMS consideration of best next steps.

The commitment to rid Medicare's quality payment program of manual updates of JSON files was written into the final rule. However, the contractors tasked with making this happen had not vetted or tested the process until after the final rule compelled them to do so. As a result, CMS contractors and stakeholders (e.g., qualified registries, providers, EMR/EHR) had to battle to create a workable submission and receipt process. CMS typically creates a "sandbox" where all vested parties can test files and communicate back and forth to improve the process. For this significant API, CMS failed to provide a sandbox, forcing all parties to independently interpret how to develop software. What was supposed to be a huge step on the path to interoperability (i.e., expedited, standard data sharing/transmission) with CMS turned into a chaotic mess.

Years have passed since the JSON challenge and qualified registries like Patient360 now successfully utilize the API. The overall outcome has been positive, as the burden of manually uploading massive volumes of data to CMS has been alleviated. Less time spent on the successful transition of data affords more time to focus on analytics and improved tools benefiting clients/providers, e.g., feedback reports, digital assessments, and UI improvements.

A key takeaway is that federal healthcare data analytics has a close relationship with policy, but policy cannot be created in a vacuum. Instead, policy should take into account the practical constraints facing those on the ground who are charged with implementing it. For smaller organizations, challenges around ensuring the consistent interpretation and application of policy might be relatively easy to overcome. For example, you might walk across the office and ask your colleague what section 8.2 means. However, in larger corporate or government entities—especially now that there is a large remote workforce—a bridge must be built to close the gap between policy and technological practicalities.

Patient360 recently tackled another challenge related to alternative payment model performance pathway programs. In 2020, CMS deployed a new iteration of one of its legacy programs, shifting from what was previously known as web interface data submission to what would be the new alternate payment model performance pathway program. This program was intended to minimize the burden on providers by reducing the number of measures they need to report and by more closely clustering specialty-related measures (e.g., cardiology, pulmonology, oncology, etc.). For providers, this change would hopefully mean that they could focus on reporting fewer measures, but that these measures would be more meaningful to their practice/specialty. For Patient360, this appeared to be an opportunity to focus on better analytics, since resources could be diverted from managing scores of unique program measures that were being retired. The new alternate payment model performance pathway program (APP) seemed too good to be true, and it was.

Similar to the API debacle, CMS rolled out the APP policy in a vacuum. While the policy itself does consider burden reduction (the famous "patients over paperwork" slogan may ring a bell), the policy gave seemingly limited consideration to data flow and behavior when interacting with specific file types. As a result, halfway through the 2020 reporting year, all stakeholders were kept in a holding pattern, waiting to learn whether they could submit data via their preferred file type, QRDA III. The lack of certainty around whether the preferred file type could be used had a negative impact on analytics software creation, since file types in this scenario are directly related to how the data can/should be assessed. Registries like Patient360 were forced to write software for this new program as if preferred file type file types would not be permitted and then wait to be pleasantly surprised if they were.

Whether policy is determined outside of your organization or from within, there are multiple steps that can be taken to ensure that policy and technology are strategically aligned. Leadership should consider the following:

- Creating a clear vision shared and valued by the entire organization
- Building a development roadmap that all leaders believe in and can support
- Including software development leaders in new policy discussions, thereby averting unintended consequences
- Mandating daily virtual huddles with leadership, especially during product revision as a result of a federal policy shift

- Deploying new software to trusted beta users willing to provide candid, constructive feedback
- Developing software in an "agile" vs. a "waterfall" process. In the agile process, software fails fast and can be rapidly fixed.

The above suggestions are not instant problem-solvers, and no process is perfect. If data analytics is the deliverable clients expect and government regulations determine format and submission details, organizations must learn how to be nimble and must connect with governmental leadership. Anticipating and successfully managing constant change is the standard modus operandi in healthcare data analytics. Thanks to the ever-expanding complexities of healthcare data analytics, job security is well-assured.

Analytics Glossary

Ad hoc reports

Ad hoc reports, also called management consultant reports, are one-off data analysis reports created to answer questions related to specific domain areas. These custom data analysis reports can be either in graphical or tabular format and are used to report on a particular metric or KPI.

Advanced analytics

Advanced analytics—often referred to as artificial intelligence (AI) or predictive and prescriptive analytics—combines computer science with robust datasets to enable problem-solving. In advanced analytics, computers are trained to perform tasks that normally require human intelligence.

Advanced analytics architect

An advanced analytics architect role within an analytics engineering function encompasses mastery in analytics, statistics and machine learning, software, and data engineering. The advanced analytics architect brings an analytical mindset and formal and rigorous software engineering best practices to the data science function while providing avenues for simultaneous amalgamation of value-driven business outcomes.

Analytics strategy

Analytics strategy is simply a blueprint that details the analytics and organizational capabilities, management systems, and resources that a business will need to reach its analytics goals, and the communication, alignment, execution, and other efforts that will also be critical in bringing an analytics project to fruition.

Anomaly detection

Anomaly detection is a category of unsupervised learning or machine learning problem used to identify patterns or events within a dataset that deviate from the norm.

Algorithms

In analytics, an algorithm is the process or set of instructions a computer follows to solve a problem or perform a calculation.

Artificial intelligence (AI)

Artificial intelligence, also known as advanced analytics, is a sophisticated branch of the analytics discipline in which machines synthesize complex data, adjust to new inputs and perform tasks, solve problems and make decisions in a manner that mimics the capabilities of the human mind.

Autonomous or augmented analytics
A form of analytics that incorporates a combination of predictive and prescriptive analytics, learns from data, and produces autonomous or semi-autonomous outcomes that require minimal inputs from human analysts.

Business problem statement
A succinct, relevant, unambiguous description of a business objective, informed by an organization's overarching goals.

Business analyst
An expert in business analysis and reporting who provides guidance that facilitates operational excellence, working with stakeholders and domain experts on organizational projects pertaining to daily business operations.

Big Data
Big Data refers to large and varied data sets that are too large and complex to be processed by traditional database management tools. Big Data technologies employ large-scale computation systems that allow parallel processing. Apache Spark and databases Apache Cassandra, Apache HBase, Apache Hive, and MongoDB are some examples. Distributed computing systems like these are scalable, fault-tolerant, and cost-effective at processing and managing high volumes of unstructured, structured, or semi-structured data from a variety of sources and formats.

Business intelligence (BI)
Business intelligence is the set of descriptive or operational analytics skills, tools and processes that make data-driven insights available—usually in the form of charts, graphs, reports, and dashboards—for business decision making

Business data silo
Business data silos are artisanal databases built for specific use cases. They are generally confined to a single business unit within an organization.

Classification
Classification is a supervised learning method that predicts outcomes based on qualitative or categorical variables. It tries to infer the output variable from a function or a machine model that generalizes the relationship based on *a set input variable*.

Dashboards
In the analytics context, a dashboard typically captures information about key business functions and operations, metrics, or KPIs at specified time intervals. This function is repeatable and automated, and the dashboard presents the periodically updated information using a combination of graphs and charts, roll-ups, and drill-downs to provide a holistic view of the health of a business.

Data analysis
The process of exploring data to find meaningful insights.

Data analysts

Experts in processing, transforming, retrieving, modeling, and deriving actionable insights from data.

Data analytics

Data analytics broadly refers to scientific thinking, experimentation, and validation techniques applied to data streams and blended with technological advancements and automation. There are three categories of data analytics: descriptive, predictive, and prescriptive.

Data context

Data context refers to the methodology and parameters under which data is gathered and provides important information to the end user. For example, a worker who consults a data table should understand why that table was created and the problem it was designed to address, how the data was derived, what it represents, and how it can be used, in order to avoid misinterpretation or misapplication of the data.

Database

A database is a collection of data that makes information accessible and electronically retrievable.

Data custodian

A data custodian is a member of an organization's data governance team who manages the technical environment in which the data resides and oversees data collection, storage and security.

Database query

A database query is a request for data from a database table or set of tables. It is formulated in a structured query language (SQL) and enables the retrieval of information in a readable form.

Data democratization

Data democratization refers to the provision and dissemination of non-sensitive organizational data to all employees at all levels within an organization, including those who do not necessarily have specialized engineering skills. Making information widely available in a usable form serves a democratizing function, enabling workers to be more effective in their jobs, to the overall benefit of the organization.

Data-driven

For organizations, being data-driven simply means making decisions, plans and goals that are informed by data rather than based on instinct, tradition or any other non-fact-based rationale.

Data engineering

Data engineering is the practice of transforming and preparing data for a variety of analytics use cases. It involves designing, building, managing and operationalizing pipelines for the collection and validation of data using defined tools and methodologies so that the data can be queried.

Data engineers
Data engineers are experts in database technology. They are responsible for configuring database environments, data collection, maintaining data pipelines, processing data, monitoring, and maintaining the performance of end-to-end data processes.

Data fabric
Data fabric is a design concept that offers a new way to power business applications with a network of information via a connected enterprise architecture. It uses data virtualization to provide API and connectors for integrating internal datastore silos and external third-party vendors.

Data foundation
Also called a unified analytics platform (UAP) or data ecosystem, a data foundation is simply the collation and assembly of raw data into a format that can be furnished as inputs to an advanced analytics model.

Data governance
Data governance consists of a set of policies and standards that govern how data is collected, stored, managed, used, and disposed of. It encompasses data infrastructure, data privacy and security, data accuracy/validity, regulatory compliance, data life cycle management and the assignment of roles to individuals and teams who are responsible for handling and overseeing an organization's data.

Data lake
A data lake is a second-generation data repository that can store an organization's structured data and a wide range of unprocessed, raw, semi-structured, and unstructured data.

Data mesh
Data mesh is a type of distributed data architecture that apportions data ownership across separate business domains. Data mesh breaks away from the traditional monolithic centralized infrastructure and its supporting centralized analytics teams, enabling individual business units to curate and maintain the data they know best.

Data preparation
Data preparation—also called data wrangling, data processing, data manipulation, data scrubbing or data cleansing—is a step in which data is arranged in the necessary format to perform analytics.

Data science (DS)
An umbrella term that refers to an amalgamation of disciplines, including mathematics, statistics, machine learning, computer science, data engineering, data and software architecture, organizational strategy, and business activities.

Data scientist
Data scientists are practitioners of data science. They are experts in building data products to solve business problems.

Data sets
A data set is a collection of data points related to a particular subject. Data sets may include information that exists in various formats and derives from disparate sources. Examples include music files, video files, tweets, documents, photos, customer information, internal organizational data and external data.

Data strategy
A data strategy is a plan that defines the tools, processes, and rules that define how an organization will manage, analyze, and act upon its business data.

Data and analytics strategy
A D&A strategy is a blueprint for using analytics. It details organizational analytics capabilities, management systems, and resources, and it outlines what data organizations should collect, maintain, and analyze to incorporate analytics and data-driven decision-making into organizational practice.

Data literacy
The ability to work with interpret and analyze data.

Data steward
A data steward performs an oversight function within an organization. A data steward is responsible for ensuring the quality and fitness for purpose of the organization's data and meta data assets.

Data wrangling
Data wrangling involves collating and assembling raw data into a format furnished as inputs to the advanced analytics model.

Data warehouse (DW)
Centralized Data Containers to collect and coalesce organizational data from various databases or transaction-processing systems.

Data virtualization
Considered a subset of data federation. Data virtualization software acts as a bridge across multiple, diverse data sources, bringing critical decision-making data together in one virtual place to fuel analytics.

Dependent variable
See *Input and output variable.*

Descriptive analytics
Descriptive analytics is the entry point in the analytics taxonomy. It seeks answers about *what is happening now or has happened in the past.* It is also referred to as operational analytics or business intelligence (BI).

Diagnostic analytics
An extension of descriptive analytics, which attempts to answer *Why did this happen?*

Embedded analytics
Embedding analytics into business processes and workflows to automate decision-making.

Exploratory data analysis (EDA)
Exploratory data analysis can be defined as an approach to summarize and visualize data using graphical techniques. It uncovers hidden structures within data, extracts information and fields, and identifies exceptions and anomalies.

Extract transport load (ETL)
ETL is the process by which data is extracted (*Extract*) from various source systems, converted (*Transform*) into a predetermined format, and stored (*Load*) in data warehouses (DWs). ETL is capable of loading torrents of data from both internal and external systems into an organizational DW in a format that is optimized to be used for analytics workloads.

Features
In the context of ML, *features* are simply variables, numeric representations of raw data tied to observable phenomena that can be measured. Identifying features from raw data and transforming and formulating the right features are necessary for building ML models. The caliber of an ML system output is highly dependent on the quality of the features extracted and selected from the raw data.

Feature-based model
Feature-based models rely heavily on humans modifying data to create new and meaningful features, which are then fed into a (simple) machine learning algorithm. This approach mixes expert knowledge with learning from data.

Functions
Functions are a way of mapping a set of inputs to a set of outputs. They perform deterministic mapping, as the same inputs will produce the same outputs. Using a simple arithmetic example, the addition function 4+4 is considered deterministic mapping since it will always yield eight as an outcome.

Full-stack data scientist
An advanced analytics practitioner with mastery in software engineering, statistics, machine learning, and analytics.

Heuristics
Strategies employed to simplify complex problems derived from expert knowledge and past experiences.

Heuristic model
A simple "rule of thumb" developed purely by humans. Usually, heuristic models are devised by those who have expert knowledge of the problem at hand.

Hypothesis testing
A method or practice used in statistics to test the validity of results in experiments.

Independent variable
See *Input and output variable.*

Industry 4.0
The name given to the fourth phase of industrial transformation, which focuses heavily on automation, artificial intelligence, machine learning, networking, cybersecurity, Big Data, the internet of things (IoT), cloud computing, data management, and other technological advancements that reduce human intervention.

Input and output variable
In mathematics, input variables and output variables are related to a function. The solution (output variable) changes as the input (variable) to a function changes. Input variables are also called cause and independent variables. Output variables are called effect and dependent variables.

Intangible assets
Intangible assets are hard-to-value assets that don't show up on balance sheets. These assets are the primary drivers of company performance that underpin the knowledge or learning economies, such as intellectual capital, research, technological innovations, intellectual property, marketing, and branding.

Internet of things (IoT)
The Internet of Things (IoT) is a network of connected devices with built-in sensors and actuators that generate raw data and talk to each other. The interconnectivity between our physical and digital worlds is called the IoT.

Key Performance Indicators (KPI)
Metrics or KPI are used for monitoring and measuring business operational and strategic activity against organizational goals and objectives. They are aggregated measurements used to capture both services and processes to enable tactical and strategic decisions.

Likelihood
Likelihood measures the frequency of event occurrence (known outcome measurements) in the past.

Machine learning (ML)
ML is considered a subset of AI. ML uses high-powered computing and mathematical models to learn and uncover hidden patterns in data without pre-programmed rules.

Management consultant reports
See *Ad hoc reports.*

Mathematical model
A system, typified by mathematical concepts to describe the underlying pattern of the input data.

Mathematical modeling
The process of developing a mathematical model is called *mathematical modeling.*

Metadata
Metadata contains information and characteristics of data, so data users understand the source of the data, how it made its way to the tables in the data warehouse, and what assumptions and business rules were applied to summarize the data.

Metrics
See Key Performance Indicators (KPI).

Model development
Model development is the process of assimilating real-world relationships—represented by data sets whose relationships and logic are defined by an algorithm—into a model.

Model fitting
Model fitting measures how well a machine learning model generalizes unseen data sets similar to the training data with which it was trained. In the fitting process, the suitable parameters can be adjusted to improve model accuracy.

Optimization
Optimization problems identify the best possible outcomes from a set of alternatives, options, and scenarios once a measure of "best" is provided, possibly subject to some sets of constraints. Optimization problems fall into the category of prescriptive analytics.

Predictive analytics
Predictive analytics is the second level in the analytics taxonomy. It addresses *what is likely to happen in the future.* Together, predictive analytics and prescriptive analytics make up what is known as advanced analytics.

Prescriptive analytics
Prescriptive analytics, the third and highest level in the analytics taxonomy, seeks to answer *what should I do now* or *how should I do it* or *what caused this to happen (root cause analysis).*

Probability
Probability is a field in mathematics that focuses on the certainty (or uncertainty) of a future event's (quantifying predictions) occurrence. It is a theoretical value often expressed in percentages.

Reporting
In analytics, reporting refers to a presentation layer that succinctly summarizes the outcome of exploratory data analysis (EDA) and advanced analytics techniques in a rich, intuitive format for decision-making. Its goal is to be consumed as is, without the need for further analysis.

Statistics
Statistics is a field in mathematics that involves the practice of data collection, exploration, and descriptive analysis to build insights with data.

Single Source of Truth (SSOT)
A Single Source of Truth is primarily a guideline that encourages all employees in an organization to use the same data.

Semi-structured data
Semi-structured data is data that does not conform to the standards of traditional structured data. Semi-structured data contains tags or other types of mark-up that help identify distinct entities within the data.

Software development life cycle (SDLC)
A framework used in software engineering to develop resilient high-quality software applications. The sequence of steps typically includes design, plan, build, test, deploy, and maintain.

Software engineers
Experts in software engineering design principles and the software development life cycle (SDLC) who can write software applications in a variety of languages.

Structured data
Structured data is predefined, formatted data also referred to as transactional data because it consists of records (*transactions*). It is stored in a table format.

Tables
Tables contain the information within a database. They are formatted in rows (records), and columns (fields).

Time series
A time series is a collection of quantitative observations evenly spaced in time and measured successively, such as daily, hourly, or in increments of minutes or seconds.

Total Addressable Market
Total addressable market (TAM) is a calculation that tracks revenue generation opportunities, identifying, for example, the maximum size of a potential market.

Training
The mathematical process of fitting a dataset to a model is called training. When a model has been trained, the data is transformed into an abstract form that summarizes the data prior to the transformation.

Unified analytics platform (UAP)
A unified analytics platform is a purpose-built platform that captures, stores and analyzes data from various sources. A UAP creates a unified data ecosystem that allows organizations to innovate rapidly, integrating engineering and data science with business.

Variables
In mathematics, a variable represents an unknown value (e.g., a number or quantity).

About the Author

Hema Seshadri, Ph.D.

Hema Seshadri started her scientific training at the prestigious Indian Institute of Technology and Indian Institute of Science, India, and moved to the United States to pursue a doctorate in organic chemistry and fulfill her dream of working in drug discovery. She was a senior scientist in the research and development wings of two successful biotech startups in the Boston area. She is the co-inventor of a patented cancer drug, *Rezurock*, licensed and marketed by Sanofi.

Pursuing her passion for advanced analytics, she completed a master's degree in computer science and pivoted to the tech industry. She started her engineering career in storage engineering, as a senior software engineer at EMC in Hopkinton, Massachusetts (MA), where she designed and developed the first advanced analytics feature in CloudIQ, a cloud analytics software as a service (SaaS) storage management software product solution. Currently, she is a senior data scientist at Akamai Technologies in Cambridge, MA, where she develops predictive and prescriptive analytics solutions for global network planning, network optimization, customer intelligence, and data center planning. She has extensive experience delivering research-based, data-driven solutions that move organizations forward. She works as an internal analytics consultant and architect on organizational analytics and business digital transformation projects and data and analytics strategy initiatives, including data fabric, data quality, and management projects. She is passionate about bringing software engineering vigor to data science practice areas. She is also involved in teaching foundational competencies related to data and analytics that allow practitioners to analyze complex problems critically. As an adjunct analytics professor at Bentley University (Waltham, MA) and Northeastern University (Boston. MA), she exposes students to the breadth, depth, versatility, and usefulness of analytics, data, software architecture and databases in problem-solving.

She mentors students and volunteers in local science fairs and programs such as the Akamai STEM Foundation, Girls Who Code, MIT Innovation Challenge, and MIT CodeIT, to encourage middle and high schoolers to pursue STEM careers. Over her career, she has authored multiple research publications and patents. She attributes her success to the cultural, adaptive, and technical challenges and experiences she had to overcome and learn from in her career.

Contributors

Colin P. Barry

Colin P. Barry is the CTO of Patient360, a market leader in providing healthcare software analytics solutions that improve quality and regulatory compliance across the continuum of care. Under his direction, Patient360 has delivered high-profile successes to clients and partners ranging from renowned provider organizations to the industry's largest healthcare IT companies, along the way gaining a reputation for excellence in engineering and clinician-centric user interface design.

Colin's professional background includes more than 25 years' experience in software design and engineering, management, and executive leadership in healthcare information systems. A passionate advocate for solving healthcare challenges with emerging technologies, Colin enjoys mentoring new young programming talent through an innovative intern program. Prior to joining Patient360, Colin served as CEO of MEDfx, a health information exchange organization.

Stephen Gatchell

As the head of the data enablement at Bose, Stephen has built the team from the ground up. Combining internal and external resources provided the institutional knowledge with key modern skills ensuring end-to-end skills for executing a data governance strategy. Developing a data strategy focused on driving measurable ROI business-driven AI, ML, and analytical use cases while ensuring privacy and security. The team is increasing data management maturity by integrating and automating data catalogs, personally identifiable information (PII), and data lineage to increase time to value for data consumption while reducing risk at an accelerated pace.

Prior to Bose, Stephen was an enterprise data strategist and chief data steward at Dell working with key internal stakeholders as well as customer engagements across data analytics, platforms and governance. Before Dell's acquisition of EMC, Stephen led an innovation team across engineering shared services supporting product go-to-market strategy and execution-focused on delivering excellence to internal stakeholders while driving down costs. Stephen was a key contributor and member of a total customer experience award-winning strategy focusing on data lake and governance as well as receiving a patent on Hierarchical Value-based Governance Architecture.

Ray Jorgensen

Ray Jorgensen is a serial entrepreneur and national healthcare reimbursement professional. A Certified Professional Coder (American Academy of Professional Coders) since 1996, Ray has become a nationally prominent speaker whose motivational style and unique perspective afford audiences unusual and thought-provoking insight into healthcare financial issues. He has personally trained thousands of providers and financial/billing professionals in all 50 states on coding, billing, and reimbursement, and he has authored several books and dozens of articles.

Early on in his career, Ray worked at Blue Cross & Blue Shield of Massachusetts and United HealthCare in hospital claims, customer service, provider relations and contracting. After a recent exit from PMG RCM & RevenueHealth, Ray holds equity positions in PMG Credentialing, Patient360 (a Medicare Quality Payment Program registry), and Kore Compliance (a cannabis-dispensary-focused business-management software platform). Ray is an avid golfer and fitness enthusiast who loves spending time with his award-winning author wife (www.TabithaLordAuthor.com) and his four beautiful kids.

Amanda Lord Darbani

Amanda Lord Darbani is the operational lead, subject matter expert, and principal of Patient360. As the P360 SME, Amanda regularly consults with CMS regarding program development and process as well as serving clients and peers who garner value from her in-depth understanding of the quality payment program (QPP) and merit-based incentive payment system (MIPS). Amanda's foundational knowledge around the PQRS program afforded her the ability to quickly synthesize the CMS 2,400-page final rule on MIPS functionality. Amanda has quickly integrated the final rule and ever-changing CMS policy into P360's day-to-day operations to assure client performance and P360 operations are maximized. Amanda is an oft-requested speaker at national conferences relating to CMS reporting and has previously presented at the Texas Osteopathic Medical Association on MIPS. She frequently authors articles for regional and national distribution. Prior to joining Patient360, Amanda held positions with higher education institutions, leading international education programs. Amanda holds a BA from the University of Rhode Island, and a BS Honors degree from the University of Newcastle, Australia. She attended graduate school at The University of Rhode Island and holds an MS in Human Development and Family Studies.

Srinivasan Sankar

Srini is a visionary leader with broad and progressive experience in data enablement strategy, analytics, and data science. Srini has demonstrated success guiding organizations to transform their businesses by leveraging mature, modern, and emerging technologies. Srini's areas of expertise include AI/machine learning, deep learning, augmented analytics, augmented data management, data mesh, blockchain in data and analytics, cognitive systems, natural language processing, data lakes, data governance, digital/ data strategy roadmap & blueprint. Srini establishes deep partnerships with the business units and aligns data strategy to business priorities, financial goals. Srini frequently speaks at MIT and other CDO, CAO, CDAO conferences, workshops, and summits. Srini currently serves as enterprise data & analytics leader for The Hanover Insurance Group in Boston.

Brahma Tangella

Brahma leads the analytics & insight function in the plasma-derived therapies (PDT) business unit at Takeda, which covers market insights, data analytics, and data science and enables digital transformation to drive differentiated experiences for donors and patients. Brahma has more than 20 years of experience across strategy & operations, consulting, technology, analytics, data science, innovation, and process improvement. His career has included positions at Dell EMC and Ernst & Young as well as in healthcare and pharma companies and government organizations. He is a business and management consultant skilled in driving transformation to develop future state architecture.

As a business and management consultant, Brahma provides thought leadership on data strategy, analytics, AI, and emerging technology. He advises senior management on critical strategy and the development of future state business vision. Brahma brings a unique perspective as a passionate innovator, technologist, and leader with an entrepreneurial mindset. He is a workshop facilitator, blogger, and speaker and a former member of the Dell technology leadership program. Brahma has co-authored one approved patent and has one pending patent.

Brahma is active in the community and enjoys photography, running, mindfulness practice, and spending time with his family. He holds a master's in computer information systems from Boston University Metropolitan College and certificates in strategy & innovation and management & leadership from MIT Sloan Executive Education. In addition, Brahma frequently participates in various workshops and summits as an expert panelist.

www.ingramcontent.com/pod-product-compliance
Lightning Source LLC
Chambersburg PA
CBHW040850110726
48005CB00001B/10